Endorsements

Stephanie Carmichael's book is authentic. We can say that because we have personally known her and Mark for over 15 years. This story unfolded before our eyes as we watched them eagerly serve and grow into faithful leaders and co-laborers.

As you read this book you will learn of a faith-filled journey that resulted in victory over cancer. We believe it will encourage and bless anyone who reads it, especially those facing possible terminal illness.

She is now being used by the Lord to bless others. Yes, our God can redeem good out of all of the battles we face. If you are feeling hopeless and discouraged, this book is for you!

John and Sonja Decker
Founders of Christ Ambassadors International
Ministry Training Institute
Bend, Oregon

Stephanie Carmichael's honest story of her personal journey in overcoming fear, as she continues to live out her faith in courage and peace, is a must-read for anyone facing a cancer diagnosis. It will bless and encourage all who read it.

Pastor Gary Burton
Westside Church South Campus
Bend, Oregon

God can use our worst situations, our most personal fears to bring us to a place of experiencing His glory. This book is an example of that. Stephanie states that cancer can provoke fear, but through her own experience she will encourage you to overcome fear as well as scripturally leading you into a life of promise. This book will help you overcome fear and become a conqueror through Jesus Christ. Scripture will be your most powerful tool, for not only cancer but in all areas of your life. You will be drawn page by page to use God's word to battle and win against fear and cancer.

Steve and Holly Taft
Pastors and Missionaries
Founders of Antioch Christian Church
Playa del Carmen, Mexico

In her book Stephanie states "We cannot lead people to a place of greater faith and victory unless we have been there ourselves." This is not a book of theories or even just good advice. Stephanie has been through the process of transforming fear into faith. Having been diagnosed with breast cancer twice, she has walked through the fire of both fear and cancer, coming out victorious over both.

Stephanie's book is a great testimony of God's faithfulness to His promises. Watching her journey as she grew in spiritual strength and authority has been a real faith builder for us personally. We believe it will do the same for all who are privileged to read her book.

John and Kathy Dolyniuk
Mentors and Trainers of Missionaries
YWAM (Youth With A Mission) Kona, Hawaii

Stephanie Carmichael

VICTORY
OVER
CANCER
AND
FEAR

Finding Peace in the Midst of the Storm

WESTBOW
PRESS®
A DIVISION OF THOMAS NELSON
& ZONDERVAN

WestBow Press books may be ordered through booksellers or by contacting:

WestBow Press
A Division of Thomas Nelson & Zondervan
1663 Liberty Drive
Bloomington, IN 47403
www.westbowpress.com
1 (866) 928-1240

ISBN: 978-1-5127-0745-8 (sc)
ISBN: 978-1-5127-0747-2 (hc)
ISBN: 978-1-5127-0746-5 (e)

Library of Congress Control Number: 2015914995

Print information available on the last page.

WestBow Press rev. date: 09/03/2015

OTHER BOOKS BY THE AUTHOR:

"The Power of Prayer Simplified"
Available at Amazon.com – Kindle E-book

Blessings of peace and renewed hope!

Stephanie Carmichael

Contents

Acknowledgements ix

Forward..xi

Introduction..xiii

Chapter 1 The Diagnosis.. 1
Chapter 2 Dealing with Fear 5
Chapter 3 Facing the Battle 11
Chapter 4 How Do You See God? 17
Chapter 5 Unmerited Favor And Grace 21
Chapter 6 Standing in the Day of Trouble 27
Chapter 7 Trusting God for More 35
Chapter 8 The Power of Prayer.. 45
Chapter 9 God's Sustaining Strength.............................. 49
Chapter 10 Activate God's Word 53
Chapter 11 Faith to Move Mountains............................... 59
Chapter 12 Intimacy With God 67
Chapter 13 Valley of the Shadow of Death 73
Chapter 14 Nevertheless – God! 77
Chapter 15 God's Ways are Higher 83
Chapter 16 Storms and Blessings...................................... 95
Chapter 17 Speak Words of Life 101
Chapter 18 Examples of Healing 107
Chapter 19 Survive and Thrive 113

Chapter 20   Why Me God? 119
Chapter 21   The Power of Praise 127
Chapter 22   Words of Life Scriptures 133
Chapter 23   Contend for Your Healing 143

Contact the Author 145

Acknowledgements

Thank you, Lord, for calling me to write this book and for being with me every step of the way. You always see the things you have planted in us, while we just see the small picture. May this book accomplish what you have in store and may it bless many who need encouragement.

A special thank you to John and Sonja Decker who are ordained Foursquare International evangelists, founders of Christ Ambassadors International, trainers of leaders and pastors worldwide and authors of the book *Doing What Jesus Did.* Without your training, support, and mentoring, this book would not have been written. Thank you for your ever constant encouragement to write, speak and teach what God speaks to my heart.

Thank you to my family – Mark my wonderful husband who reads all of my writings not once, but many times over. Your loving support is so important to me. To my son, James, who gave me valuable input in the editing process and to my daughter, Julie, who reads and edits every talk I have written and this book - it means so much to have you as editors! To my daughter, Gina and son in law Jeremy, thank you for your loving encouragement and for our grandbaby Lily.

Forward

If we live long enough, we eventually come to realize that life can seem like a series of battles or challenges. We get through the challenges and think we are settled when suddenly out of left field we take another hit and are struck down by a new set of challenges.

The vast majorities of us go through life from challenge to challenge and do our best to use our wisdom, life experiences, resources and friends to help us get through. But sometimes we find ourselves thrown into the middle of circumstances that are way over our heads. We can't see around it, we can't go through it or climb over it, and no matter how hard we try, we can't make it go away.

Sometimes it takes a life threatening crisis, a bad doctor's report or a great loss of some kind to let us see that we need help greater than ourselves to get through it.

This book is about a season of great challenges that I had to walk through brought on by breast cancer, and the healing process that taught me how to live life fearless and victorious!

Introduction

The breast cancer diagnosis came on the heels of some other great losses in our family. My husband's mother died of ovarian cancer in September 2001, which was devastating to all of us. But while we were still mourning that loss, my mother died in August 2002 after open heart surgery.

From that point in 2002 we started seriously seeking God for comfort, peace and emotional healing. Our lives had been like a sinking ship with holes in the sides where sorrow leaked through, but Jesus became our new strength, our comfort and the healer of our broken hearts.

My husband and I became involved in ministry training classes at our church as leaders and became very involved in teaching others about the power of God in our everyday lives. We were still learning more while we were helping our students learn to rely on God and have greater faith. One of the exercises of this class is learning how to pray to heal the sick.

This cancer diagnosis was a very scary and bad report, but it actually caused me to dig deeper in my relationship with God. It gave a whole new meaning to praying to heal the sick, as I was now in serious need of healing.

I knew that many people died of cancer lesser than mine, but I also believed that God can heal all things and that He would sustain me.

God always meets us at our point of need if we will ask Him to. My need for the healing power of God became so great, but He was faithful to meet me every step of the way.

During the three years after our mother's had died, I had been reading the bible faithfully for peace and comfort. The words of God were already embedded in my heart and mind, but little did I know there was so much more.

There is a richer, deeper and more intimate relationship with God that can only be realized when we are desperate for His touch. Not everyone goes there, but if we choose to we will get to know our loving heavenly Father in such a beautiful way that we are forever ruined for the ordinary!

I chose this path and the purpose of this book is to share it with you. This pathway is open for all of us and, if you are hungry for more of God, just know that He is hungry for a deeper relationship with you.

Chapter 1

The Diagnosis

As I thought about writing this book, I thought of all the people who have received a bad report at the doctor's office and the fear that runs through them when they hear the words "you have cancer" or "you have a terminal illness." The doctor goes on to tell them what kind of cancer or disease they have and the statistics about survival rates. He lays out the plan of attack to give the best chance possible for survival, and then they sit in stunned silence and utter shock.

In June 2005, the day after my son's fourteenth birthday, my doctor told me that my test had come back positive and that the huge lump in my breast was cancerous. My greatest fear had been confirmed. I remember sitting there in disbelief. How could this have happened to me? This was something you hear about other people going through, not me!

FEAR COMES KNOCKING

As my surgeon spoke about the various aspects of my condition, my mind started to whirl with thoughts of the cancer in my body, and my heart was pounding so hard in my chest that I could almost hear it. I was so glad my husband was with me because I only heard half of what was said. The doctor told me that I had the option of having both breasts removed, which was what his wife had chosen to do. Both breasts!! Seriously?? I didn't want to have one removed; after all, isn't that part of what made me a woman? In my mind, having a mastectomy was one of the worst things that could happen to a woman.

When I was in my early twenties, a couple of older women I knew had breast cancer. After their mastectomies and chemotherapy, they never were the same. They seemed to have lost a spark that they once had.

Eventually, they both died of cancer, and it was such a tragedy. After that, I never wanted to hear about breast cancer, as it had become an underlying fear at the back of my mind. I remember avoiding magazine articles about breast cancer just so I wouldn't have to imagine it.

Now, here I sat on this surgeon's table in a sterile environment hearing my worst fears come to life. This just could not be happening. He tried to reassure me that I was not going to die while telling me that I had an invasive, aggressive type of cancer.

The surgeon kept on speaking about the choices I had, which I really didn't see as choices but just cold hard facts. They ranged from possibly doing chemotherapy first to try to shrink the tumor and save the breast to having the mastectomy and then chemotherapy or having both breasts removed and being done with it. Oh yes, and then having chemotherapy.

One thing I did hear was, "Breast cancer is slow growing, so it has probably been growing for five years or more to get to this size." How could that happen when I went for my mammograms regularly? My palms were sweaty, my teeth were clenched and I couldn't wait to get out of there!

TIME FOR PROCESSING

I asked the doctor if I could wait a few weeks since this cancer was slow growing, and he said there was no harm in doing that. When we got home, I booked a family trip to Hawaii. I really needed some time to process all of this, and I wanted our younger kids, who were seventeen and fourteen, to remember that summer as the year we got to go to Hawaii and not the year Mom had breast cancer. Looking back on it, I now can see that it was my way of coping with the bad news as well as a time for my family to be together.

Although I had faith that God could heal anything, I was still processing this news. I knew that God was bigger than cancer but I also knew I could not battle this giant alone. I was powerless.

Our whole family was thrown into shock once again. Our kids had been doing much better in school, and their hearts were finally healing from the loss of both of their grandmas and now their mom had breast cancer. I could only imagine how they felt at the thought of losing me, especially after experiencing the death of both their grandmas. This broke my heart.

The only way I could help them was to be strong and not let cancer beat me down. But how could I do that when cancer was so much bigger than me? I knew I could not be strong enough on my own but I also believed that God could strengthen me. It was then that I made my decision to lean on God for strength and knew that He would get my family through too.

COMING BACK TO REALITY

One thing about a vacation to Hawaii is that it is a nice escape from reality, but you always have to come back. When my doctor further discussed the options with me, none of them were what I wanted to hear. It turned out that a lumpectomy was not possible, as the tumor was so large that he would have had to remove half of my breast. Thank God for my husband, Mark, who was by my side for each doctor visit and every procedure. He was my rock and prayed with me through every situation that arose.

The enemy of fear had rushed into my mind like a flood and started chaotic thinking, but I knew that God's Word says,

> *"When the enemy rushes in like a flood the Spirit of the Lord will lift up a standard against him."*
>
> (Isaiah 59:19)

I claimed this Scripture as my own. My faith in the healing power of God was greater than the problem, and I made a decision to put this whole situation into His mighty hands as I prayed for His help. I was powerless to solve this problem.

God could take away the cancer with a single touch and I would be healed. But the easy way out is not always the best way for us. God uses everything for good, even cancer, and I have always tried to look for the good in what I call the "seemingly bad."

Chapter 2

Dealing with Fear

The Bible says that God is with us always and He will never leave or forsake us.

"God's love for us is from everlasting to everlasting"
(Psalm 103:17)

"I will never leave you nor forsake you"
(Deuteronomy 31:6)

"For I am with you always to the very end of the age."
(Matthew 28:20)

This was a time of testing these promises.

It was no accident that my husband and I got into the ministry classes at church two years before, as cancer was growing in my body even then. God was preparing us for what He knew was coming. Our God is a sovereign God; all knowing, all powerful, all wise, everywhere present and at all times on our side. He promises that if we seek Him with all of our hearts, minds, and strength, He will not fail us.

Over the years, my husband and I have established the early morning hours as our prayer and devotion time with God. We both have faith in the healing power of God and have come to realize that He heals in many ways - through doctors, medicine, and also through miraculous healing. He knows which kind of healing we need, and as we pray, He heals us in all the ways we need it from the inside out.

After much prayer and faith building, the lump was still there, but my faith was becoming greater than fear. Through this cancer season, I realized that it is much easier to have faith for healing when I am praying for someone else and it is much harder to have faith for my own healing.

Fortunately, we had made many wonderful friends in our weekly prayer group that we attended and also in our classes, and they all surrounded us with love, support and prayer. Several of them were at the hospital with us praying as I underwent surgery.

My surgeon, who was also a Christian, told me that if there was any sign of cancer in the lymph nodes, we would have to do a mastectomy soon. I had already prayed and made the decision to have the mastectomy if necessary.

MORE BAD NEWS

The first surgery was to check for cancer in the axillary lymph nodes under my armpit. Not only was cancer found in them but also in the next two levels of lymph nodes, there was cancer in eleven out of twenty-two nodes.

As I lay in the recovery area after my surgery, I remember my surgeon leaning down face to face with me and he told me that there was definitely cancer in my lymph nodes and that I would need a mastectomy within a week.

One would have to be superhuman not to experience fear with that kind of doctor's report. Even with great faith in God, fear can still overwhelm us. But I discovered that what I did with fear was extremely important to my health and peace of mind. Even though I had been developing a foundation of faith, fear gripped my heart and my mind was filled with "what if" thoughts.

"WHAT IF" THINKING

Fear of the unknown is one of the worst fears we can face. With cancer, or any deadly disease fear thoughts can be almost as destructive as the disease.

The "what ifs" start rolling through our minds like a hamster running on a wheel. These kinds of thoughts can run rampant through our minds.

What if I'm not strong enough to do this? What if the chemo makes me sicker than I already am? What if I go through all of this and die anyway? What if I don't get to see my children grow up? What if this fear infiltrates my children's lives? How will it affect them if I die? What if my husband can't handle all of this stress? Will our family fall apart?

Try as we may to stop them ourselves, fear thoughts turn into circular thinking and we always end up back at square one with the "what if" questions. When we cannot see the outcome of a terrible diagnosis, we suddenly realize that we are definitely not in control of it and that makes us feel out of control and fearful.

In my case, I had nowhere to turn but to God. I had experienced the power of God in my life to bring me peace in other situations, and I knew He had the power to deliver me into peace if I would just give Him my fear. This isn't something that happens automatically or a one-time decision; it is something that is built up and maintained on a daily basis over time.

It gave me a choice either to live in fear and let it devour my every waking moment, or take it to God and lay it in His hands. Making the choice to give it to God is almost easier when we are out of options. However, we must choose to give up fear if we are going to gain peace! This became a season of learning to speak God's Word over my own life to conquer fear.

STRENGTH IN THE MIDST OF CANCER

I can remember desperately opening the bible to seek strength to face the days ahead of me. Not knowing for certain if I was going to live or die was a heavy burden to carry. But God was my continual source of peace and comfort.

The everyday things that we take for granted suddenly had new meaning. I knew my children still needed me; my husband and I had always been joined at the hip and he needed me. Cancer caused fear in everyone in our household.

I began to realize that how I handled this fearful season was going to affect everyone in our family, and I made a decision to walk in faith and to be an example to my children. Without God to lean on, without God's Word to count on each day, without prayer - faith would have been impossible.

LEARNING TO TRUST GOD'S WAYS

During this cancer season, I learned valuable lessons about how much God loves me and how personal He wants to be in my life. Most importantly, I learned how to speak words of life over my situation and how to pray effective prayers for myself and my family.

This season definitely was not a waste of time. In fact, in retrospect I must say I am actually grateful for the things that the Lord has shown me about Himself, His nature and His unfailing love for me that I would not have known otherwise.

Most of the time, I try to be an optimist, the "glass half-full" kind of person. Life has dealt me some heavy blows, and I have learned through tough times to call it the "seemingly bad" because something good always comes from it. However, that viewpoint did not work so well this time as the "seemingly bad" was so very bad that I could not see a light at the end of the long dark tunnel.

No! This was definitely a season of learning to lean on God when I was weak and gain a new strength that came from a power greater than me. The good news is that God was there ready and waiting for me to call on Him, and I can guarantee that He is there for you too!

FAITH IN SOMETHING GREATER

My normal default mode was worry and then anxiety – even without cancer. I grew up in a dysfunctional home and this kind of thinking is hard to escape, even though I know better. It is a battle. I am not naturally a person of great faith, but it grew in me during a time when I really needed it. It grew into faith that I would live and not die because of God's promises. Faith is the greatest gift that we can cultivate during times when we are powerless about the outcome of a very fearful season. Yet sometimes it can be the hardest thing to grasp. I learned that great faith must be cultivated over a period of time and with the help of God.

Chapter 3

Facing the Battle

Make no mistake about it, cancer is a full on battle! For me personally it was very much like an uphill battle. Facing the diagnosis of aggressive breast cancer made me take stock of my life. What was important and what could I just let slide away from me. My children, husband and family were my main concern. They needed me and I needed to fight for them as much as for myself. My family is probably the one main thing that gave me a reason to persevere in trying times and not give up.

Fear and oppression seem to naturally come with a cancer diagnosis. Fear of the unknown is one of the most powerful enemies that I faced, especially in the middle of the night when I would suddenly wake up and the house was so quiet. I would look in on my children sleeping and the fear of them losing their mother would overtake me. Fear that I would not get to see them grow into adults or see them graduate from high school, college and get married. They still needed me as I needed them.

Whether it is cancer or some other life threatening diagnosis, fear usually accompanies it. So the question is how do we battle and win? What are my weapons for battle? We always need weapons, if we are going to fight! And how do we fight a foe that brings such fear, anxiety, and oppression with it? God knew we would have battles to fight; He gave us these words,

> *"For the weapons of our warfare are not of the flesh,*
> *but have divine power to destroy strongholds."*
>
> (2 Corinthians 10:4 ESV)

The only weapon I had was the sword of God's Word! I had read a little book called **Healed of Cancer** by Dodie Osteen, and in it she talked about how she spoke God's Word into her life when she was sent home to die of cancer. Her situation was hopeless and her doctor said she just had a short time to live – that was in 1981. This was now 2005 and she was still alive and all cancer had been eradicated from her body!

Sometimes we need to start with other people's faith which comes from hearing their story. After reading her testimony of how God healed her terminal cancer, it ignited a new seed of faith in me, a new starting point on which to build greater faith.

SPEAKING WORDS OF LIFE

What we speak and think has everything to do with victory. The things we focus on 24/7 begin to manifest in our minds, hearts and emotions. It eventually becomes our perspective on life. But we can choose to change the course we are on and that starts with speaking words of life.

> *"As a man thinketh in His heart, so is he."*
>
> (Proverbs 23:7 KJV)

I started applying the principle of speaking God's Words to my own circumstances. What was I saying and believing about my own life, about what the doctor said about me? Learning to speak words of life started me down the true road to faith and peace for this season.

Daily I started seeking God's Word in the bible searching for things He was saying to me for my circumstances, and faith began to rise up in me! Don't ask me how that happens, it just does. I began to realize that God really does meet us at our point of need. He gives us exactly what we need to battle and win against any foe.

He gave me Scriptures to stand on such as in the story of Joshua,

> *"Every place on which the sole of your foot treads I have given it to you," and "Be strong and courageous, do not tremble or be dismayed for the Lord your God is with you."*
>
> (Joshua 1:3, 9)

God spoke these words to Joshua as he was handed the daunting task of leading all of the Israelites into the Promised Land after the death of Moses. They had to battle their way through many enemies, and they were victorious because the mighty hand of God was with them.

IT TAKES PRACTICE

Changing the way we speak and think about our circumstances takes some discipline. I practiced personalizing God's Word and inserted myself into the Scriptures.

He says be strong and courageous because He will be with me every step of the way! I began to see and believe that nothing is more powerful than my Father God and no one more compassionate than my Savior Jesus. No foe can overtake me if He is on my side. I began to get a deeper understanding that Jesus died on the cross not only for my sins and mistakes but also for my sickness and disease.

When Jesus went to the cross for us, He was beaten to within an inch of His life. He had stripes on His back from the whips. Scripture says *"and by His stripes we were healed."* (1 Peter 2:24) I started speaking this for my own life *"By His stripes I am healed!"* until I actually started believing it.

> *"Be to me a rock of habitation to which I may continually come; you have given commandment to save me, for You are my rock and my fortress!"*
>
> (Psalm 71:3)

I began to craft these Scriptures into a personal prayer daily like this:

> **"Lord you said that You are my rock of habitation and that you have given command to save me. Lord I take you at your word and I claim that for my own life. By your stripes I am healed."**

I spoke these simple faith-filled statements throughout the day and night. It became easier the more I read the bible and memorized passages.

Psalm 91 is still a mainstay for me; it became a place to dwell in day and night. It says

> *"He who dwells in the secret place of the Most High*
> *shall abide under the shadow of the Almighty."*
>
> *(Psalm 91:1)*

When I pray in this manner, I embody and become what that Psalm is speaking of. Now I pray daily that I shall abide under the shadow of the Almighty and that destruction must pass me by. The Psalm goes on to say

> *"I will say of the Lord my refuge and my fortress,*
> *my God in whom I trust; for it is He who delivers you*
> *from the snare of the trapper and from the deadly*
> *pestilence. He will cover you with His feathers and*
> *under His wings you may take refuge."*
>
> (Psalm 91:2-3)

The shelter of the God most High is where I took refuge when thoughts of fear and anxiety threatened to encompass me.

After I started speaking God's promises over my life and cancer, I noticed that fear would simply evaporate. I also came to understand that faith and peace are huge weapons that God gave me to keep me strong and courageous during this great battle.

Chapter 4

How Do You See God?

Before we continue, let me ask you a question. Who is God to you and how do you perceive Him? Some people have a long distance view of God. He is the Creator of everything but not involved personally in their lives. Some see God as a life energy or life force that connects everything together. Some people refer to God as "the universe," as in the universe must have done this for me or wanted me to end up here.

Many people view God as an old man father figure sitting high above His creation judging them at every turn; a Divine Creator not interested in their little personal lives and not a personal God. Some people see God as judgmental, harsh, critical of their every move and unapproachable. It is hard for them to see God as loving, caring and someone who wants to heal them.

If we read the bible with an open heart and mind seeking to know who God is for us, we will gain new insight. He reveals Himself to us through our hearts. Jesus came to clarify false concepts and to teach us about the Father. Jesus says

"You will worship the Lord in spirit and in truth, for God is spirit!"

(John 4:23-24)

God is not an old man sitting on a cloud judging the world, but God is Spirit! God is all knowing, everywhere present at all times, all powerful Creator of the heavens and earth. God is omniscient (all knowing); God is omnipotent (all powerful); God is omnipresent (everywhere present). Jesus told us God is spirit, this is how He can be everywhere present at all times involved in every detail of our lives. He also said when we pray we are to say *"Our Father who art in heaven."* (Matthew 6:9) Jesus, His Son, revealed that God is our personal heavenly Father.

John, an apostle of Jesus, tells us that *"God is Love,"* (1 John 4:8) not just loving but the great big capital "L" Love. The reason He desires our worship is because worship comes from our hearts and He wants to connect with our hearts. Our little finite love connects with the big infinite love and we have Divine connection with our creator God! The Apostle Paul said

> *"Be anxious for nothing but in everything make your requests known to God."*
>
> (Philippians 4:6)

He was saying do not sit around in worry and anxiety, but pray with faith that God will answer us. These Scriptures gave me a starting point for building a foundation of faith from which to pray.

LEARNING TO ABIDE IN HIM

> *"I am the true vine; abide in Me and I in you for the branch cannot bear fruit by itself."*
>
> (John 15:4)

*"If my words abide in you ask whatever you wish in
my name and it will be done for you."*

(John 15:7)

These words show us that Jesus is a very approachable Savior who is loving, full of mercy and grace. He invites us to abide in Him, dwell with Him, learn His words so we may ask the Father anything in His name and it will be done for us.

Jesus bridged the gap between us and the Father! He let us know that we are not meant to stand alone. There is help for us, if we will abide in Him and dwell in a safe place with Him. This is very comforting to those who are in need.

Jesus invites those who have Him in their hearts to ask anything in His name and it will be done. But how do we know how to ask? It is written throughout the bible; we are to ask according to God's will for us. His will for us is to rescue, heal, restore and transform us into the best version of ourselves.

HOW APPROACHABLE IS GOD?

Many people believe they must clean up their dirty living before they can go into His presence. God never said that, man did and still does! That is a terrible lie which keeps so many people on the outskirts of the transforming power of God! Jesus did not say anything remotely like that; in fact, He hung out with the tax collectors, sinners and prostitutes – the most despised people of their time, rather than the so called religious men. Jesus wants you just the way you are, and He will help you clean up your life.

His work on the cross crushed all sin. He sacrificed Himself on our behalf, and when He did unmerited mercy, unmerited grace and forgiveness was released into the whole world for each of us. Unmerited means there is nothing you can do to earn it. When you ask Jesus to be the Lord and Savior of your life, unmerited grace and favor of God also comes as a free gift! Without God we are simply powerless to make a permanent transformation of our lives.

TOO SINFUL TO PRAY

It is the loving Divine connection with God that empowers us to make positive changes in our lives, to do the things that we are powerless to do on our own! I have had many people ask me to pray for them or for a loved one and say to me "I'm a sinful man (or woman) and I don't feel I can pray to God." This is another terrible lie that is widely believed and a misconception of who Jesus is in our lives. God is waiting to hear your voice call to Him.

The very name of Jesus (Immanuel) means "God with us." The name of Jesus carries the resurrection power of God to heal you of sickness, restore you from all sin, addictions, infirmities and life's situations. The transforming power of Christ in us is the most powerful force for good that we can embrace. If you are going to battle a giant like cancer, terminal illness or addictions you need to know this. You can't do it alone! God is ready and willing to go to battle on your behalf.

Don't let a bad experience from the past keep you from a personal relationship with our loving Savior. Don't let someone else's judgment, criticism or harshness keep you from enjoying an abundant life with Christ. God has all of the answers you need for living life abundantly!

Chapter 5

Unmerited Favor And Grace

God's unmerited grace, favor and mercy empowers us to live life victoriously! It sets us free from sin and oppression. Our part is to ask for help and confess that we need a Savior to wash us clean and receive God's love.

Did you know that God loves you just the way you are with all your faults and mistakes? He sacrificed His only Son on the cross for all the sins of the world so that ALL may be saved; you are not an outsider! Jesus tells us in his own words,

> *"For God so loved the world that He gave His only Son, that whoever believes in Him shall not perish but have everlasting life"*
>
> (John 3:16)

> *"Truly, truly I say to you, whoever hears my word and believes Him who sent me has eternal life."*
>
> (John 5:24)

Notice the simplicity of these two statements. We complicate it with our minds, but Jesus spoke it simply and plainly; simple yet powerful truths.

God loves us, He sent His Son to tell the world about His love, mercy and grace available to us. Jesus demonstrated God's love by healing and comforting people and by teaching us about Divine LOVE of the Father.

Wouldn't we be wise to believe the words of Jesus, not the words of men? If you find it hard to believe that God loves you just the way you are and wants to pour out His love into your life, read the book of John written by a man who walked with Jesus and watched Him heal the multitudes. John speaks about the transforming love of Jesus for all of us. Whatever the cause, we can read the truth in the bible and see God's compassion for us.

> **"For God did not send the Son into the world to judge the world, but that the world might be saved through Him."**
>
> (John 3:17)

In the bible, we see places where God rescues His beloved people from impossible circumstances. We see that Jesus came to demonstrate that love personally when He came for us.

Jesus says,

> **"The thief comes to steal, kill and destroy; I have come that they may have life and have it more abundantly."**
>
> (John 10:10)

I call cancer a thief that wants to rob us of our very lives! These Scriptures are meant to encourage us that God is on our side no matter what comes against us.

Everyone who came into the presence of Jesus with even a morsel of faith was healed. His actions speak of His deep love for us. It says throughout the bible *"He healed them all."*

Do you need to be rescued from your circumstances? Is there something you are facing that is too big for you? God is willing and able to help you, but you must ask Him. We need to set a foundation from which to pray and grow in faith.

MAKE TIME FOR GOD

Sometimes we are so busy with our everyday lives and we think we've got it covered; until one day a crisis hits. Life has a way of bringing us to turning points. Many times it is the turning point which makes us willing to turn our hearts to God. He is continually inviting us, but He is also a gentleman. He will not go where He is not wanted. God yearns for you His beloved child; He weeps for you when you are hurt.

He tells us in Psalms *"For God is near to the broken hearted and saves those who are crushed in spirit."* (Psalm 34:18) Are you crushed in spirit? God wants to soothe your soul, to take you lovingly in His arms and comfort you. Jesus said *"My sheep hear my voice."* (John 10:27) He sees you as His little lamb, and He is the Good Shepherd who wants to comfort you. Soften your heart, open your arms and receive the comfort, peace and calm confidence that Jesus wants you to have.

HOW DOES GOD HEAL?

God heals us in different ways. As I have said, I would surely have desired to be healed instantly. But in His wisdom He set me aside during that season of cancer, while He had my attention, so I could learn who He really is to me personally. He drew me into an intimate time while I was seeking Him with all my heart, mind and strength. Through reading His words and promises, through prayer and meditation, through prayers prayed over me by others time and time again, I slowly gained a new vision of who God truly is for me.

Before I was healed of the cancer that invaded my body, I was healed of fear, anxiety, false concepts, anger, bitterness and unforgiveness. That was quite a package I was carrying around. But when I opened the door through prayer and invited God into my daily life, I gave Him access to heal me fully! I no longer was afraid of dying; I knew for sure that I would be with Jesus if I died and that my loved ones would be cared for by a God who loves them. The knowledge of that brought me a deep and abiding peace.

With all of this in mind, let me say that I am no more special than you. This kind of healing and comfort is available for you right now. Invite Jesus into your heart and see for yourself the comfort, light and life that He will bring. He will give new direction to your life, and He will cause all things to work together for good for you. He is speaking to your heart right this minute!

Pray this simple prayer and invite Jesus to come into your heart:

"Jesus, come into my heart. Forgive me for the things I have said and done that were wrong. Wash me clean of my mistakes and give me a fresh new start. Thank you, Jesus, for being the Lord and Savior of my life. Amen"

Jesus invites us

> *"Come unto me ALL who are weary and heavy laden*
> *and I will give you rest"*
>
> (Matthew 11:28)

He means ALL! He didn't look out in the crowd and say "You come, but not you" He said ALL! And what are we heavy laden with? All the burdens of the world, sickness, cancer, disease, doctors' reports of all kinds, all of our bad habits, addictions, things that cause oppression in our lives, finances, broken relationships, lost love. He invites us to lay it all down at the foot of His cross and He will lift it off of our shoulders.

THE FINAL PIECE OF THE PUZZLE

> *Taste and see that the Lord is good; how blessed is the*
> *man who takes refuge in Him."*
>
> (Psalm 34:8)

There is a God sized hole in all of us. We try to fill it up with other stuff, but nothing brings complete or lasting satisfaction. We remain restless and unsatisfied as we continue to search for that one thing that will bring completion to our lives but to no avail.

Years ago I can remember thinking, if only we can qualify to get that house I will be happy or when this happens or that happens I will finally be fulfilled. Not so! Those things came and went but my life didn't really change. I was still the same on the inside.

Friends, it is not a job or a place or a new love that will bring a feeling of being complete, satisfied and whole. No! None of these things fills that void inside. It is a deep and abiding relationship with God through His Son Jesus that fills the hole, nothing else can do it. Once you have this truth, everything in your life is better. You can be content right where you are. Thank God I found Him before cancer came into my life!

That empty hole is reserved for God only. It's the last puzzle piece that you have been missing in your life. When it is finally snapped into place in your heart, you will see the whole picture of your life more clearly.

You will gain a new peace and contentment and won't need to rush to things and people for your happiness. God sized JOY will replace sorrow and discontent no matter what your circumstances are. This is the place from which we can battle cancer victoriously. This is the secret place we go to receive peace, comfort and healing.

FRESH PERSPECTIVE

We can start to see our lives with a God view and can experience life abundantly. All the peace, comfort and rest that we long for will be available through the love and mercy of Christ in us.

As I read the bible with a new fresh perspective and especially the New Testament I began to see all of the places that mention God's love for me. Jesus said He came to fulfill the Law of Moses, because we cannot do it on our own. He did it for us because He loves us, it is done! You don't have to do another thing to earn His love.

These words are meant to encourage you to reach out to God with a heightened awareness of who He truly is for you and that He wants to heal you. As you start to read and speak God's promises into your own life and circumstances, the words themselves will help you gain more faith. We will talk more about how in later chapters.

Chapter 6

Standing in the Day of Trouble

One of the things I learned to love most about the Old Testament is the stories of actual people who lived through hard times and the examples of how God rescued them. It was during this time of really seeking to know God in a deeper way that these stories came alive for me, and I could see how to personally apply them to my circumstances.

At that time I did not like reading the Old Testament much because of the wars and bloodshed. But when reading it from the perspective of cancer attacking my body and threatening my life, my mind and heart perceived these battles and victories on a personal level.

One of the key stories that I could identify with is found in 2 Chronicles 20. King Jehoshaphat was the king of Judah and its surrounding territories including Jerusalem. One day he received a message about three huge armies much stronger than his army coming to attack and annihilate them. His first response was fear. *"Jehoshaphat was afraid ..."* but his next choice was key to how this story ends. *"He turned His attention to seek the Lord and proclaimed a fast throughout all of Judah."* (Verse 3)

This was his game plan for victory. He was powerless, but he had faith that God would help them.

When the king made this proclamation throughout all the land the people listened; they came from all the cities and the countryside. They gathered together in one huge corporate gathering in a spirit of unity to seek the Lord God to save them. This was powerful and humbling at the same time. He prayed a humble prayer in front of all those gathered.

> *"O Lord, the God of our fathers, are You not God in the heavens? And are You not ruler over all the kingdoms of the nations? Power and might are in Your hand so that no one can stand against you."*
>
> (Verse 6)

He went on reminding the Lord about promises that He had made to Judah in the past and he laid out the report before God and his fear of destruction from these great enemies. He ended with this statement of faith

> *"O our God, will You not judge them? For we are powerless before this great multitude who are coming against us; nor do we know what to do, but our eyes are on You."*
>
> (Verse 12)

It was a humble prayer by a great king, praying to the King of Kings.

I saw myself in this story! The multitudes of cancer cells were attacking me and I was powerless to stop it, but I called out to God to save me.

Was God silent when King Jehoshaphat and all of Judah prayed that humble prayer? No! One of the Levites (holy men of God) heard God's answer and spoke it out.

"Listen all Judah and the inhabitants of Jerusalem and King Jehoshaphat – thus says the Lord to you; 'Do not fear or be dismayed because of this great multitude, for the battle is not yours but God's."

(Verse 15)

He gave them instruction to go down and meet the enemy and further said

"You need not fight in this battle; position yourselves, stand and see the salvation of the Lord on your behalf Judah and Jerusalem. Do not fear or be dismayed tomorrow go out to face them for the Lord is with you."

(Verse 17)

Reading this story at precisely the right time while I dealt with cancer spoke to my heart; and it increased my faith. I took this example of how God fights on our behalf and proclaimed it for myself:

"I will face my enemy cancer without fear because the Lord is with me to fight this battle!" I realized in that moment that the battle was not mine but God's! My job was to humble my heart, surrender myself and this cancer to the Lord and position myself for victory, through faith in a power greater than myself.

Upon hearing this word from the Lord, King Jehoshaphat bowed his head with his face to the ground and all Judah and the inhabitants of Jerusalem fell down before the Lord and began worshiping. They all worshiped and praised the Lord loudly in one accord, in agreement with each other believing that God would deliver them.

We don't always like to humble ourselves because we see it as a sign of weakness. But actually, being humble before the Lord and asking for His help is a place of great strength. It opens the door for God to move in a great way on our behalf.

We may have a certain amount of strength naturally, we may have great powers of logic and gifting of wisdom, but that's not always enough. If we will humbly ask the Lord for His strength in place of ours, He will multiply what we do have and lift us high above our circumstances!

They arose in the morning and Jehoshaphat spoke words of faith to his people:

> **"Listen to me, O Judah and inhabitants of Jerusalem put your trust in the Lord your God and you will be established."**

> (Verse 20)

Then he appointed the people who were known for being worshippers to go before the army of Judah singing praises to God, and look what happened next.

> **"As they went out they sang 'Give thanks to the Lord for His lovingkindness is everlasting. When they began singing and praising, the Lord set ambushes**

> *against the sons of Ammon, Moab and Mount Seir,*
> *who had come against Judah; so they were routed."*
>
> (Vs 21-22)

Now the army of Judah came to the lookout of the wilderness, *"they looked toward the multitude, and behold, they were corpses lying on the ground and no one had escaped."* (Vs 24) They didn't have to fight in that battle, but they worshipped the Lord and He fought it for them. The worship partnered with what God wanted to do for them and caused divine intervention on their behalf.

Does God have power to annihilate our huge enemy cancer? Yes, I definitely believe He does! But the question is, will we let him? When we are in a desperate place with the odds stacked against us, God really has a chance to speak to our hearts. He led me to this story to show that He is willing and able to wipe away my enemies.

WHO OR WHAT IS THE ENEMY?

We must identify our enemy and know what we are battling in order to pray with wisdom. It's not just cancer that is my enemy; it's the destructive emotions of stress, fear, and chaotic thoughts that are also my enemies.

Because of this life threatening disease and the emotions that came with cancer, it made me willing to really go deeper with God. He showed me through His Scriptures that He was and still is a God that will not only help us fight our strongest, hardest battles, but He will actually fight them for us, if we will position ourselves for the victory by humbling our hearts and asking for help.

REPOSITION YOURSELF FOR VICTORY

The next question is always how do I do this in my life? How can I be repositioned for victory? The answer is little by little, getting to know God through His word daily and prayerfully asking for revelation of His words personally. You will start to learn the truth about God for yourself and it will open your heart to receive His help. Faith opens the door for God to come in, and faith is grown by reading and hearing God's Word.

> *"So then faith comes by hearing and hearing by the word of God."*
>
> (Romans 10:17)

Faith grows as we read, speak and pray the Word of God. There are other tools that helped me grow in faith. I listened to many CDs, went to conferences, read books about faith and healing. Also I had worship music on all the time at home and in my car. There are many good sources out there that can help you to grow your faith. The important thing is keep your mind filled with positive God thoughts and not focused on the problem at hand.

I didn't start this journey with great faith that God would defeat my enemy cancer, but somewhere along my journey through the cancer season my faith grew to enormous heights. It was not all at once, but again it was little by little. We don't start at the end, we can only start where we are and grow from there; but God loves a willing heart. Lay down your fears and anxiety daily at the foot of the cross and allow God to take them from you.

I was fortunate that I was surrounded by Christian friends who had great faith that God would heal me. I received prayer weekly from one group of friends or another, and I was also on the prayer team at church, and I still am today.

God brought me many people to pray for who had diseases including cancer. Sometimes I would actually see them get healed while I still had the tumor in my breast. But I believe that God had strategically placed me in that faith filled environment to grow my faith and to heal me.

Chapter 7

Trusting God for More

We can't lead people to a place of greater faith and victory unless we have been there ourselves. There is peace available for us in the midst of the storm. There are many levels of healing - physical, emotional, mental and spiritual. God wants us to experience them all, but it is usually a journey and a season of healing when we are set apart for God, as we allow Him to gain access to our hearts. The greater the need, the more desperate we are, the more opportunity there is for God to draw closer to us.

> *"Draw near to me and I will show you great and mighty things which you do not know."*
>
> (Jeremiah 33:3)

I am convinced that God knew I would come through this process victoriously and that I would share my story with others to help them grow in faith. The bible is filled with stories of how God met people at their point of need in desperate times. These stories gave me great examples of how God can turn my fear into victory. He will do it for you too!

Learning that I have a choice of how I will respond to cancer, fear, anxiety and stress was really a revelation for me and a turning point in my faith. I continued to study the bible intent on seeing myself in these stories of wars, battles and victories in seemingly impossible circumstances; I learned that nothing is impossible with God. When you are in the trenches yourself and need encouragement, God knows exactly how to help you.

In the story of Jehoshaphat it says that when he was afraid and turned to the Lord for help, *"Jehoshaphat bowed his head with his face to the ground."* (2 Chronicles 20:18) Then in my thoughts I heard God say "praise and worship the Lord." I went into the bedroom that morning and lay down on the floor with my face on the ground and wept at my Lord's feet. Humbly I surrendered all of this battle to Him because I knew I was powerless over it.

God said to my heart and mind *"I have not given you a spirit of fear, but of power, love and a sound mind."* (2 Timothy 1:7) As I lay this burden at the foot of the cross and cried out to the Lord "save me I can't do this alone" peace took the place of fear. Right then at that moment, I realized the power of God's peace to eradicate fear.

GOD'S TIMING

Interestingly, the day that the cancer report came was the same day that we usually go to our prayer group. We went that night as usual and shared the doctor's report. Everyone gathered around me and laid a hand on me to pray. I can only say that the comfort I received was truly from God, as He spoke words of encouragement to me through our praying friends. Our good friends and mentors from our ministry training class, John and Sonja Decker, had a confirming Scripture for me and a comforting word.

Sonja said "Stephanie, the Lord says that He has not given you a spirit of fear, but of power, love and a sound mind."

My confidence started to rise as I heard the exact same Scripture that God had given me that morning.

John said "The Lord sees you as already healed, but it's not going to appear immediately. He is going to put you through a process of healing. He wants you to cooperate with the doctors and do everything they say to do and He (the Lord) is going to use everything for good. God sees you as already healed, but He will do things in you that would never happen otherwise."

These were powerful words prayed over me, and I have come to believe that the Lord speaks through our hearts and minds as well as through those who are praying for us. We seek Him and He comforts us in this way. Those words have stayed with me since that day, I still claim them today!

At the end of 2 Chronicles 20 in the story of Jehoshaphat, great blessing was poured out on everyone.

> *"After the enemy was defeated, so much blessing was poured onto the people of Judah; they took the spoils and the riches, more than they could carry."*
>
> (2 Chronicles 20:25)

The blessing comes out of our dry hard times, after the battle is won. As we seek God in our darkest hour, He transforms our troubles into blessings. None of our pain is wasted, God uses everything for good. New faith, hope and strength are born in us and we become courageous!

Since this season of breast cancer, I have had so many opportunities to encourage people, to pray and minister to the broken hearted and the sick. Because of this cancer season and what I learned, I became a speaker for Stonecroft Ministries where I continue to share my stories of faith, hope and the love with others. This blesses me beyond belief!

RESCUE ME LORD!

This was a season of learning how to contend for healing daily and sometimes from hour to hour. I went through very scary procedures much like facing the giants that King David had to face in the bible.

About two weeks after the mastectomy they started me on the most toxic chemo drugs available. The first infusion took seven hours because it was given drop by drop. This drug is so toxic that if one drop touches the tissue outside the vein it will kill it and it will never grow back. They called it the "Red Devil," very reassuring. After they started giving me that drug, my doctor decided it was a good idea to add a port in my chest for easier access to all of the drugs they were going to pump into me over the next months.

From my perspective this was like facing another giant. Everything was unfamiliar and scary. We have all heard stories of what chemo does to people, and I saw it firsthand all around me. Going into the chemo room for infusion is not a happy place. You see all kinds of fear and varying degrees of side effects on the people there. I always took my bible and read during the long chemo sessions. The following story has spoken to my heart over and over again as an example of trusting in God and I hope it helps you too.

CRY FOR HELP

King David, the author of many Psalms, knew God intimately. He was called "a man after God's heart." In 2 Samuel 22 after a battle with a huge enemy army where David almost lost his life, he sings a song to God praising Him for rescuing him from death. It starts out:

> *"The Lord is my rock and my fortress and my deliverer;*
> *My God, my rock in whom I take refuge, my shield*
> *and the horn of my salvation, my stronghold and my*
> *refuge; My savior, You save me from violence."*
>
> (2 Samuel 22:2-3)

Cancer and disease are strong enemies that attack our bodies with violence. They carry death and destruction with them. But when we meet that attack by speaking words of faith from these Scriptures into our own circumstances, peace starts to permeate our mind and our soul is refreshed. Getting rid of stress and fear is very important for healing to occur.

> *"For the waves of death encompassed me; the torrents*
> *of destruction overwhelmed me; the cords of the grave*
> *surrounded me the snares of death confronted me."*
>
> (Verse 5-6)

King David reflected on his dire circumstances, and that they were too great for him to handle alone. I thought about this and saw how it applied to my own battle with cancer. When we pray Scripture and speak words of life into our circumstances, we don't deny that the circumstances exist, but we do acknowledge that God is greater than any foe we may face. King David continues,

> *"In my distress I called upon the Lord, yes, I cried to my God; and from His temple He heard my voice and my cry for help came into His ears."*
>
> (Verse 7)

David is stating that he knows that God heard his cries for help and that his prayers reached God's ears. God hears you too! Do you believe God hears your prayers?

Jesus told us

> *"Do not let your heart be troubled; believe in God, believe also in Me."*
>
> (John 14:1)

> *"Whatever you ask in My name, that will I do, so that the Father may be glorified in the Son. If you ask anything in My name, I will do it."*
>
> (John 14:13)

This is a powerful statement of who Jesus is and what He is willing to do for us! This was instruction that He gave before He was crucified. All throughout Scripture, be it the Old or New Testament, God the Father, God the Son and God the Spirit are revealed as being loving, healing, comforting, ready to restore us.

Do we logically understand all of it? No! We cannot comprehend all of it, but it is still the truth. Just because we may not believe it doesn't change the truth. But we are also told in several places in

Scripture that if we pray according to God's will for us, it will be done for us.

HOW DO WE KNOW WHAT TO PRAY?

As we meditate on God's Word day and night, mutter it under our breath and speak it into our hearts, it becomes a part of who we are. Then we will know the will of God, because it is written in His word. If we do this, we will eventually come to realize that God wants to connect with our hearts! God is love and He wants only what is good for you His beloved one.

We are assured of God's love and protection over us in the book of Isaiah.

> *"Do not fear for I am with you; do not anxiously look about you for I am your God. I will strengthen you, surely I will help you, surely I will uphold you with My righteous right hand."*
>
> (Isaiah 41:10)

These words of love and encouragement spoke to my heart and they have become words that I call on often. They speak of the relationship God wants to have with us, one much like a child and father.

When I give my talks and speak of these Scriptures, invariably people come up to me after the talk and say "Where are these Scriptures, I really need to know them? I want to buy your book." God's Word spoken out loud to others impacts their hearts. I see tears on people's cheeks as they hear how much God loves them. God broke my heart for what breaks His heart.

This is the reason why I share my story, because people need to know the power of speaking God's Word into their lives. They need to know that Father God and His Son Jesus truly love all of us and want to prosper us! These words are eternal; they are ageless, timeless and very much alive and active for our circumstances today.

Ask anyone who has had an encounter with God; He can change things for good in an instant! He can use everything you are going through right now to work for good in your life and to build faith, trust and character.

This is a time to turn our faces toward the Lord of all creation and to worship Him in Spirit and in truth; to call upon Him and to know that He will move on our behalf. When I go to my speaking engagements, I am constantly surprised at how many Christians do not even read the bible. We are simply too busy or distracted as a culture to take the time daily to do devotions. Yet the key to our spiritual, mental and emotional freedom is hidden within the Scripture; such a paradox! It does take discipline, but the rewards are great! It is easier to start small. Just read a paragraph per day from the book of John, and you will find yourself wanting more of God's Word in your life.

"Draw near to God and He will draw near to you."

(James 4:8 ESV)

This is God's invitation to spend time in His presence.

Many times it seems to take a catastrophic event in our lives which causes us to stop what we are doing and turn to God with abandon. But take heart, it is never too late. God uses the seemingly bad to turn things around for good. No matter what your circumstances are today, God can turn it around for good.

One thing I came to believe after spending so much time in God's presence during the cancer season is that nothing is too big for God! Jesus is the name above all names, He is my healer, He is greater and stronger than cancer, greater than any enemy and nothing that I face is too powerful for Him.

My hope is that this book will encourage you to get more involved in reading Scripture daily, and you will eventually hear all that God has to say to you. My prayer is that the Scriptures in this book will give you a head start for the battle that you are presently facing, and you will see the importance of being in God's Word daily because it has the power to transform your life.

Chapter 8

The Power of Prayer

In previous chapters, I have spoken of cancer as a battle. It is something that we who have had it can agree on; and we need to fight and battle to win. Whenever I hear that someone I know of has cancer, it just makes me all the more determined to finish this book. For we can fight it with drugs, chemotherapy, surgery and doctors, but there is another dimension in which we can fight it, and that is the spiritual dimension through prayer.

The power of prayer to manifest healing of all kinds has been recorded throughout time all the way back to biblical times. Praying Scripture (God's Divine word) over situations and people is a powerful way to pray. It calls upon God's own words spoken to mankind and it is a prayer of agreement about what God has already said He will do for us!

My oncologist once told me "We can fight cancer with drugs, surgery and chemotherapy, but we don't heal. Something greater than us does the healing." He is a man of science who did not seem to have an active belief in God, yet he knew that he did not have the ability to heal me himself.

FIGHT TO WIN!

During my time of fighting cancer, this became a huge part of how I battled it. I experienced first-hand the actual power of God's Word which carries healing in it.

When I was contending for my own healing and life, I learned how to pray in a more powerful way about my situation. I also learned how and when to rest in the Lord and allow Him to strengthen me. I would like to share a couple of personal stories with you that showed me the power of God being released into my situation.

As I mentioned previously, my husband and I were leaders in helping train people in ministry at our church. That class met every Monday night for a full nine months and we were there four hours each session. My husband and I also were on the prayer team and were involved in training classes and prayer after services.

Anyone who has gone through aggressive chemotherapy and radiation sessions knows how tired and worn down we get from those procedures, much less getting over major surgery simultaneously. I prayed about it and asked the Lord if I should step out of these ministries; and the answer I got came to me as I was reading the bible.

> *"Surely I will strengthen you, surely I will help you*
> *and I will uphold you with my righteous right hand."*
> (Isaiah 41:10)

I also read in another book that God says *"Pray for others that you may be healed."* (James 5:16) This is usually the way that God speaks to me, through His own word and it rings true in my spirit as confirmation. The prayer team gave me the opportunity to pray for others every week.

When my leaders encouraged me that it was okay to take this season off from these ministries, I told them that I believed I was supposed to remain active in them. They actually turned out to be a lifeline for me in building more faith and trust in the Lord, which I would need to draw upon in the days ahead. The battle of cancer seemed like a season without end, and on my own I grew weak and weary, but God knew where I belonged.

The lymph node dissection and mastectomy surgeries were performed just a week or so before our new ministry class was to begin. After having two major surgeries with general anesthetic one week apart, I should have been too tired to attend the kick off BBQ, but three days after my mastectomy surgery I felt good enough to attend; not just good enough but actually energetic!

Everyone marveled that I was there and that I looked so lively! This was just the beginning of God actually showing me in practical ways that He was going to strengthen me physically during this time.

Throughout the six months of intensive chemotherapy I did experience the weakness and the wrung out feeling that chemo causes. However, when it came time for me to go to church and be on the prayer team or be in the ministry class, God gave me the strength to go. It was a supernatural strength that I physically did not have in me. I would say a little prayer asking that He would strengthen me. Then by faith I would get up off the sofa and walk down the hall to get ready, and by the time I was dressed I was fully energized. I kid you not!

In the beginning I was amazed that God would do this so quickly for me, but I remembered that He said He would strengthen me when I was weak and that He would heal me. This was a time of training for me, a time of learning to trust in God completely and of learning how to pray and ask Him for help. I literally went from being bundled up in a blanket on the sofa so tired from it all, to being transformed into an energetic woman who could go out and take part in the ministries.

People started commenting to me about this saying they were amazed at how well I was doing and that I was a "walking testimony" to them about how God was healing me. At that point it really didn't hit me fully about what God was doing in me, but I continually received comments like this.

One of our friends in the ministry class that year was a surgeon, and he kept telling me how remarkable it was that I was able to function normally considering the aggressive treatment I was undergoing. He knew how the procedures usually affect patients and each week he would comment on it.

Week after week I spent a great deal of time in prayer and I could feel my strength come to me when I had to go out. It was like a cloak of strength was being wrapped around me. When I called upon the Lord to strengthen me for the class, my prayer went something like this.

"Lord you said you would be my strength when I am weak, so right now, by faith, I am asking for your strength to fill me up. I am getting up and walking down the hall knowing that when I am finished getting ready I will be fully energized. Thank you, Lord, for healing me and for your strength. In Jesus name, Amen"

It was that simple but it was prayed in faith, a new faith that was growing in me!

Chapter 9

God's Sustaining Strength

The next round of chemotherapy lay ahead of me. What I knew going in is that Taxol can cause many bad side effects among them hair loss (but I was already bald), the ever prevalent nausea, weakness, weakening of the immune system, nerve pain, pain in arms, back and legs, heart damage and damage to organs, "chemo brain" etc. What I was not prepared for was the crash cart that they brought by my side as they prepared to administer the drug. I asked the nurse why the crash cart was there and she said this drug was known to have possible effects of cardiac arrest, convulsions and a list of other possible side effects after just one drop. That was alarming!

Honestly, my first reaction was shock and fear, and it took time to gather myself and speak words of life over my circumstances. But one thing I did over and over during the long cancer season was to pray with each person who was going to perform a procedure on me. They always agreed and it brought me peace. I prayed for the nurse who was going to administer the Taxol and for God to protect my body from bad side effects. My husband was with me as a support and he gripped my hand tightly before the nurse inserted the needle. Then I told her I was ready to start.

Rather than allowing fear thoughts to dominate my mind, I closed my eyes and prayed silently during the treatment, **"Lord** *you are my light and salvation, what shall I fear? Lord you are the defense of my life, what shall I dread? For in the day of trouble you will hide me in your tabernacle; in the secret place of your tent you will hide me. You will set me high upon a rock out of harm's way. Lord I'm asking you to hide me now,"* my version of Psalm 27. I would meditate on the words that were in my heart and then fear always left me. This was the practical application of the power of God's Word applied to my situation.

> *"Lord you have rescued my soul from death, my eyes from tears and my feet from stumbling."*
>
> (Psalm 116:8)

I now trust these words.

IN THE CHEMO ROOM

The infusion took hours, seven hours the first time as it was administered slowly, drop by drop, then five hours per treatment weekly after that. I did not want to go to the chemo room. Each week I had to go and each week I had to battle fear. There is no joy in the chemo room; it is a very heavy place. Everyone is in a room in large lounge chairs receiving various forms of chemo infusion; everyone there is in a battle for their very lives. I made it a point to speak with whoever was next to me receiving treatment and tried to encourage them with the little book *Healed of Cancer* that I mentioned earlier. Most people were glad to receive it, only one person rejected it.

This room was a battlefield where I spent many days, weeks and months going through one kind of chemo or another. Sometimes we don't get to choose our circumstances, but we do have a choice of how we are going to walk through them. My choice was to allow God to increase my faith daily as I called on Him and He continually met me at my point of need. God's strength in me helped me over every hurdle that was too great for me.

Chapter 10

Activate God's Word

There is truly power in speaking God's Word into your life. How do we know this is true? The bible speaks continuously about God's Word. God says,

> *"So shall my word be that goes forth from My mouth;*
> *it shall not return to Me void, but it shall prosper in*
> *the thing whereto I sent it"*
>
> (Isaiah 55:11)

> *"He watches over His word to perform it."*
>
> (Jeremiah 1:12)

That means He is watching for His word to be released by faith and that He will move on it.

If we speak God's Words back to him, we pray the perfect prayer and we pray God's will into our lives. As we speak God's Words and promises into our own life, it is activated by faith and our faith begins to line up with the truth of His Words to us.

Further, the bible says

> *"For the word of God is living and active, sharper than any two-edged sword, and piercing to the division of soul and of spirit, of joints and marrow and discerning the thoughts and intentions of the heart."*
>
> (Hebrews 4:12)

This says that God's Word is alive today and more powerful than ever! Learning this truth helped me to see the importance of praying His word back to him. God is listening for your voice and He instantly recognizes His Words. When God answers our prayers, it is the very substance of His word becoming manifest in our circumstances.

Amazingly we see that God invites us concerning the works of His hands.

> *"Thus says the Lord, the Holy One of Israel and his Maker, ask Me of things to come concerning my sons, and concerning the work of my hands you command me."*
>
> (Isaiah 55:11)

Speaking God's promises back to Him commands the work of His hands. It calls forth His promises for our lives. God is saying trust me, have faith in me, speak my words out in faith and My hands will go to work on your behalf.

FAITH IN THE CHEMO ROOM

I haven't talked to one person going through cancer who enjoyed going for chemo. It is something we endure for the greater good of our healing. I believe God works through our prayers mixed with doctors and other procedures. Sometimes God gives a miraculous healing, but many times it is a journey of faith that we must walk through.

Whenever it was time to go for my chemo sessions, I learned to call on God's promises to sustain me. I would call a couple of friends and let them know I was on my way to chemo and ask them to please pray against fear and anxiety for me.

Then I prayed for myself, always out loud which helped me to hear back what I was speaking and it helped my faith to rise up. By the time I arrived for my treatment, I felt stronger and I believed that Jesus was with me and my Heavenly Father was protecting me at all times.

My prayers went something like this.

"Lord you said you are my light and salvation; the very defense of my life, whom or what shall I fear? Lord, take this fear and anxiety from me. Be to me a rock and my strong shield; for it is you who goes before me to crush my enemies under my feet. You, Lord, give me victory over cancer and fear. Nothing is stronger than My God who loves and cares for me. Let your light shine in the darkness and deliver me from fear. I choose to stand in the shadow of the God most high until destruction passes by. No weapon forged against me shall prosper, because my God is stronger than anything I may face. Thank you, Lord, for watching over me and protecting me from destruction. I trust only in you. In Jesus name I pray this, Amen." (Psalm 27,

2 Samuel 22:3, Psalm 57:1, Isaiah 54:17) I learned how to combine Scriptures for the perfect prayer.

As I continued praying in this way, God always sustained me in peace and I sat in the chemo chair in calm confidence that He was fighting on my behalf even at that moment.

ASK, SEEK, KNOCK

Jesus said

> *"Ask and it will be given to you, seek and you will find, knock and it will be opened to you."*
>
> (Luke 11:9)

Jesus was teaching His disciples the principles of prayer and the power of asking the Father. God is telling us that we must ask according to His will and it will be done for us. How do we know His will? It's in the bible and we see it plainly written from cover to cover. His will for you is always good! He listens for a heart that is praying and asking; knocking and seeking. God is good to His word, faithful to answer our prayers in many creative ways.

> *"Let us hold fast to the confession of our hope without wavering, for He who promised is faithful."*
>
> (Hebrews 10:23)

"Without wavering" is the key to receiving what God promises.

> *"God's ways are higher than our ways, His thoughts higher than our thoughts."*
>
> (Isaiah 55:8)

This shows us that when we pray, God will answer in the way that is best for us. Sometimes our eyes are so focused on the problem that we don't perceive answered prayer starting to happen. At first I just wanted God to take out the tumor from my body; that would be the easy, most likely way for me to be healed, according to my own way of thinking.

Friends and even strangers prayed over me and many times I heard **"God is healing you, but He wants to heal other things in you before you see it physically. He is taking you through a process; you are being set aside during a season of getting to know Him intimately."**

That did not sound like what I had in mind! We want things instantly, but then I remembered that His ways are higher than my ways and I decided to submit my heart and soul to the full process. I became a willing participant in what God wanted to do in my life and future. I remembered that my heavenly Father knows the beginning from the end and He has plans for my life that I cannot see. I learned to totally trust in Him without putting my fingers in the middle of what He wanted to do. When we plant a seed, it will not grow if we keep uncovering it each day to look. I felt like God was saying to me **"Be patient, who says I'm not answering your prayer, have faith and trust in me."**

Chapter 11

Faith to Move Mountains

God's Word is mighty and powerful, it carries the power to heal our bodies, our circumstances and releases divine reversal of things set in motion against us.

Jesus further said to His disciples

> *"If you have faith, you will speak to this mountain and command it to be uprooted and cast into the sea, and it will be done for you."*
>
> (Matthew 21:21)

In fact, much of Jesus' teachings demonstrated how to command healing. He even said

> *"He who believes in Me, the works that I do, he will do also; and greater works than these he will do; because I go to the Father"*
>
> (John 14:12)

> *"Ask the Father anything in my name and He will do it."*
>
> (John 16:23)

Jesus would not have said it if it wasn't true. If we believe part of what Jesus said, then we must believe all of what He said, for He came to reveal truth to us. *"For you shall know the truth and the truth will set you free."* (John 8:32) If we can logically figure out how God does everything, then He's not God. Our finite minds cannot comprehend the Infinite, which is where faith comes into it.

How do we proclaim God's Word back to Him? Pray like this:

"Lord you said to speak to the mountain and it will be uprooted and cast out into the sea. So Lord I speak to this mountain called cancer, 'Be uprooted from my body and be cast out away from me.' Cancer has no right to my body; my body is a temple for the living Spirit of God and my enemy cancer is under my feet! Thank you Lord for your word which says You are my healer, You say that I am healed. I call heaven to touch earth in my body and command healing in Jesus name. Thank you Lord, I believe and I receive. Amen" (Mark 11:23, 1 Corinthians 6:19, Luke 20:43, Psalm 18:39 Exodus 15:26, Matthew 6:10) Combined Scriptures

There is a battle that goes on between our head and our heart, our mind and our emotions. Speaking God's Word into our lives and circumstances causes a shifting in our minds and hearts. It sets things in motion to work for good in our lives. It causes us to start to line up with the truth of what God says. *"You shall know the truth and the truth will set you free,"* is a concept given to us by God so we will know that He truly is causing all things to work together for our good.

As we speak God's Word into our circumstances day by day, week by week it causes God's hand to move on our behalf. We can speak His word with authority knowing that His written word to us is truth. So in faith, as we proclaim God's Word over our circumstances, we are causing them to line up with the truth of how God sees our circumstances. As we speak God's Words back to Him, we are praying for His will in our lives. God will always answer the prayer that speaks His words back to Him in faith.

Again God says *"for I am watching over My word to perform it."* (Jeremiah 1:12) He delivers on His word and deposits it into our lives where it is needed. His word supersedes all circumstances that we may be going through. God's Word says

"I am the Lord who heals you."

(Exodus 15:26)

He wouldn't say that if it wasn't the truth. Truth is eternal, it was true 6,000 years ago when He first revealed it to man in Exodus 15:26, and it was demonstrated by His son Jesus when He healed ALL who came to him asking for healing.

"Power went out from Him and He healed them all."

(Luke 6:19)

God's holy word is the truth over cancer, over any disease even terminal illness. God watches over His word to perform it, and He says yes!

Prayer:

"Lord you said You are my healer, you said you watch over your word to perform it. In faith I'm asking you now to deliver me from cancer and its destruction, from the fallout of cancer which is fear, doubt, anxiety, weakness and oppression. Lord, cleanse my heart and mind so that I may receive the healing

you have for me on many levels in my life. You are my strong tower and I ask you to strengthen me in my weakness. Help me go on your strength when I become weary. Let fear melt away in the presence of your love and peace. Thank you, Lord, for answering me. Amen"

Know this truth; there is power in speaking God's Word into your life. I continued to speak His Word every day into my life and circumstances, and I still do to this day! God gave me new words to pray every day as I read the bible. He would prompt me and say to my heart **"This word is for you, this is how I see you."** He would speak words of love, healing and kindness to me, and I finally learned firsthand the power of praying God's Words back to Him.

HEALING IN THE FIRE

Another testimony I would like to share with you is about when I went through radiation therapy. After months of chemotherapy, they gave me a rest for about a week and then started me on six weeks of daily radiation therapy. Radiation treatments can cause extreme tiredness, radiation burns on the skin, nausea and other side effects. Because I had cancer in the lymph nodes of my armpit, they gave me extra radiation in my chest wall, my armpit, shoulder and up through my collar bone. Again it was a more aggressive tactic to stay ahead of additional cancer in the lymph nodes.

To say the least, I was not happy about the prospects of this next phase of treatment. But once again I gained encouragement from the Lord, and He led me to many Scriptures which gave me strength and peace to go through the process.

After about 22 sessions of daily radiation, my skin on my chest became burned, raw and weepy. They had to stop treatment as I had second degree burns with blisters. They gave me some medicine to apply daily and we prayed for healing.

After about five days, the doctor told me that we couldn't wait any longer and that I had to resume the radiation treatments or I would have to start all over again. I had eight more sessions to go, and my skin was still raw and sore. But I told him I was willing to start again, if it was absolutely necessary.

When I went for the next session, the technician commented that my skin still looked burned and raw. I told him what the doctor had said and that I had decided to go ahead with the procedure.

During this time I was scared, fearful of pain, scarring and infection; but mostly it was fear of the terrible pain I had already experienced. I renewed my prayers to the Lord and in a leap of faith I asked Him to heal my skin even though I was getting more radiation. I asked Him to cover me under His shadow and protect me and heal my skin completely.

An amazing thing happened! After eight more sessions of intensive daily radiation therapy my skin was completely healed!! It was soft and smooth and was a normal color. On the last day of radiation, my technician said to me "Wait a minute! Your skin was red and raw when we started these last eight treatments and now it looks healed with no irritation. How does that happen? What are you putting on it?" My response was joyful and I said "That is the power of prayer!" I told him how I had asked God to heal me even though I was getting more treatment. His response was "That's amazing!" and he looked very surprised. He said he had never seen anything like it before!

ENDURING STRENGTH

During this whole time of treatment, the strength of God enabled me to function as a leader in the Monday night classes, serve in church on the prayer teams, as well as attend Tuesday and Thursday night prayer groups for continual prayer for healing.

In one of the prayer meetings, a young woman prayed over me and said that she saw a picture of a Holy Fire burning through me from my head to my feet and that God said He was healing every area that needed healing including my hair. She called it accelerated healing. I was still completely bald at the time and had no hair on my body at all, not even eyelashes or eyebrows. My oncologist had just told me that morning that it would take about six weeks for peach fuzz to start growing on my head.

SIX DAYS after that prayer, I realized that I had peach fuzz growing on my head! I was shocked to see it! I was also going in to see my oncologist again; and he was also shocked to see that six days after my last chemotherapy treatment I already had peach fuzz growing on my head. He said "I've never seen this before! It usually takes at least six weeks for hair to start to grow." I told him that many people were praying for me and "that's the power of prayer." He just shook his head perplexed by what he saw.

These may sound like small things to others, but they were profound to me. In fact, it's part of what shaped me into a woman of great faith that God can do anything! It birthed new belief of who God is in my life. Because of what God did in my life during that long seemingly endless season of breast cancer, I feel the need to share my story with others to encourage them to believe that God will heal them.

Many people ask me for prayer because of the evidence they see of God in my life. During the cancer season I prayed for a number of people who were healed either immediately or within a week of the prayer. I learned to trust God and His timing because the bible says

> **"His ways are higher than our ways and His thoughts higher than our thoughts."**
>
> (Isaiah 55:9)

But I also learned that God hears every prayer that I speak, even small ones, and He has taught me how to see answered prayer all around me.

Some things we just take for granted or we think it's a coincidence, but I have come to recognize answered prayer and feel so blessed every time I see it. I now believe that if I prayed it and then I see it happen, it is answered prayer.

Chapter 12

Intimacy With God

God wants to enfold you in His loving arms, He wants to soothe you and let you know that He is there for you in every circumstance. His Word speaks of His great love for you

> *"Come unto me all who are weary and heavy laden and I will give you rest. Take my yoke upon you for my yoke is easy and my burden is light."*
>
> (Matthew 11:28)

This invitation was spoken by our compassionate Savior, Jesus. He wants to take your heavy burdens of fear, anxiety and sorrow and exchange it for His yoke of love, peace and joy. He holds His arms out to us saying *"Come and follow me, come and trust me; give that burden to me."*

God is always speaking to us, ever near, closer than breathing and nearer than hands and feet. He is always speaking to us and we just need to learn how to tune our ear to hear Him. He speaks words of love and light and He longs for you to sit in His presence and rest in Him.

He speaks to our minds and hearts continuously. Sometimes we call it a hunch, or we say we just knew we were supposed to do this or that. Some people call it their conscience, knowing the difference between right and wrong; or a chance encounter with someone who changes their life forever. But all of it is God speaking to His people; it is God causing all things to work together for good.

> *"The Lord is near to the broken hearted and saves those who are crushed in spirit."*
>
> (Isaiah 34:18)

> *"Draw near to God and He will draw near to you"*
>
> (James 4:8)

> *"You have collected all my tears in your bottle"*
>
> (Psalm 56:8 NLT)

These Scriptures speak of an intimacy with God our Father. You are His beloved child and He longs to comfort you. He sent His son Jesus to speak truth to the world and to die for the sins of the world, so we don't have to.

If you knew all of this was true for sure without a doubt, wouldn't you run straight into the arms of your heavenly Father? Sometimes we must go on the faith of someone else until our own faith can grow. It gives us a starting point for faith.

LET YOUR FAITH GROW

When asked how much faith it takes to experience what God has for us, Jesus replied

> *"If you have faith the size of a grain of mustard seed"*
>
> (Matthew 17:20)

A mustard seed is the tiniest of seeds in the world, yet it can grow a huge bushy tree that brings shelter to birds and little animals. Mustard seed faith is where most of us begin, but if we persevere God can grow that faith greater than we can imagine.

To get through a season of cancer, disease or some other terminal illness takes a lot of faith. But we don't start at the end, we can only start right where we are and grow from there. A man asked Jesus to heal his son by asking *"If you can, please heal my son."* Jesus replied *"IF I can? All things are possible to him who believes."* The man replied *"I do believe, help my unbelief."* Jesus then healed his son. (Mark 9:22-24) I believe He also grew the man's faith as his son was healed.

That can be our prayer too. **"Jesus I believe (kind of) but help my unbelief; I want to believe more, help me to grow in faith."** God will always meet you right where your belief and your point of understanding are and grow more faith.

> *"For the eyes of the Lord move to and fro throughout the earth that He may strongly support those whose heart is completely His."*
>
> (2 Chronicles 16:9)

God wants to reveal Himself to you His beloved. Whatever you may have believed in the past, the truth is that God really does love you and wants to heal you on every level. Years ago, I didn't believe the way I do now; I too had a mustard seed of faith. But God showed me that He truly loves me and protects me. He showed me that I am worth saving and that He values my life. Now I know for sure that it's all true!

TRUST GOD'S PERSPECTIVE

In the beginning of this cancer season, I would have really liked for God to heal me instantly from breast cancer. I would have chosen not to go through a long arduous process. But today I would not give up what I gained through that two and a half year process for anything.

If I had been healed instantly, I would not be writing this book of encouragement because I would never have experienced God first hand. I would never have felt His healing touch in the same way that I did during this cancer season. His living Word in the bible became like a love letter to my soul, and I am forever changed! I can only encourage you to delve into His promises and begin to claim them for yourself.

If you would like to have a closer relationship with God, pray this prayer with me inviting Jesus to dwell in your heart. Say **"Jesus, come into my heart. Forgive me for things I have said and done that were wrong. Wash me clean of my sins and give me a fresh new start. Be the Lord and Savior of my life. Thank you Jesus, Amen"**

It's a simple yet powerful prayer and when prayed sincerely, it will change your life for the better forever. You will also begin to understand the bible better and you will gain new revelation and understanding of what God's Word means for you personally.

UNMERITED MERCY

Why would God be so gracious to us? The bible says

> *"But God is so rich in mercy, and He loved us so much,*
> *that even though we were dead because of our sins,*

> *He gave us life when He raised Christ from the dead.*
> *It is only by God's grace that you have been saved!"*
>
> (Ephesians 2:4-5)

Even when we had our backs to Him, God loved us. Even when we denied Him, God loved us. His love is so powerful and so great that it overcame our denial of Him and continues to draw us to Him. Even when we didn't deserve it, God poured out his unmerited grace and mercy for us through His Son Jesus.

God wants to transform your life for good. His will for you is to walk in freedom from darkness. He sent forth His light to overcome the darkness. Jesus said

> *"I am the Light of the world. He who follows me will*
> *not walk in darkness."*
>
> (John 8:12)

God watches over His word to perform it. Now that we know this truth shouldn't we start speaking His words of love, healing and grace into our own lives? The end of the book will have more Scriptures that you can speak into your life that will raise your faith.

A GOD OF DETAILS

> *"Indeed, the very hairs of your head are all numbered."*
>
> (Luke 12:7)

> *"Are not two sparrows sold for a penny? Yet not one of*
> *them will fall to the ground outside the Father's care.*
> *And even the very hairs of your head are numbered.*

71

> **So do not be afraid; you are worth more than many sparrows."**
>
> (Matthew 10:29)

Going through cancer helped me to see that God is interested in every detail in my life. God led me to Scriptures that I needed to sustain me that spoke of life and healing. We must open our minds to understand that, if God sees every sparrow that falls and He provides abundantly for all the needs of His creation, He actually cares what happens to all of us.

This thought struck me as I was reading the book of Numbers chapter 4; I suddenly realized that God is a God of details. The book of Numbers gave detailed instruction to the Israelites as to how to set up the tabernacle in the wilderness. Everything was perfectly ordered and described in great detail.

Every tent peg had a place, every fork and utensil for the altar was described. He told Moses how to build the tabernacle and how to tear it down and get it ready for moving. As I read about how detailed the instructions were for handling the tabernacle, I felt that God whispered in my ear **"Stephanie, I know every single detail in your life and I care about it. Come to me and ask me for even the tiniest detail, and I will answer you because I love you"**

This is a huge concept to wrap our minds around! God sees every detail in your life and He cares about it. He invites us in to ask Him for everything and to turn to Him for all of our needs, while growing in a new intimacy with Him!

Chapter 13

Valley of the Shadow of Death

"Yea, though I walk through the valley of the shadow of death, I will fear no evil for you are with me. Your rod and your staff they comfort me"

(Psalm 23:4)

At some point in our lives, most of us have heard this scripture. It sounds ominous, it looks ominous and it is fearful when we find ourselves in that valley; but I found out that we must do what the Psalm says **"walk through the valley!"** The valley of the shadow of death is not a place to sit down and stay in, but a place to keep walking through until we reach the other side.

It is perfectly understandable to sit down and weep in the valley of the shadow of death, but at some point we must lift our heads up and look around. This is when we must shift our eyes to Jesus who is waiting there in the valley of the shadow and He says to us

"Do not fear for I am with you, do not anxiously look about you for I am your God. I will strengthen you."

(Isaiah 41:10)

This is an invitation from the Lord of heaven and earth to give Him our cares, worries and anxiety. He wants to take it from you if you will let go of it. Give Him your anxiety, fear, depression, disease, addictions; give it all to Him and ask for help and restoration.

> *"For I will restore health unto thee, and I will heal thee of thy wounds"*
>
> (Jeremiah 30:17 KJV)

The way we make it through the valley of the shadow of death is to get up, place our eyes on Jesus and start walking, one foot in front of the other. We must not sit down and stay in that valley of the shadow of death for it will overtake us.

GOD'S VIEW OF THE VALLEY

Let's examine this Scripture a little more. It is called the "shadow of the death." This means it is only a shadow not reality and that we can step out from under it. It is not something tangible, but it is made up of fear thoughts such as; fear of dying, fear of the procedures, the toll on your life and the havoc it will wreck on your body. But, just because those things are all prevalent and go along with the cancer diagnosis, it doesn't mean that we are compelled to go through the process in fear and trembling.

God wants to strengthen you, He wants to rescue you from the valley of the shadow of death and give you victory. But the question always remains, will we let Him? We only see what's in front of us, but God sees the whole picture! He has an aerial view of our lives. God's perspective is higher than ours; He sees where we are going to be five years down the road. We can only see today, but we must choose to engage our will to trust God's way so we may gain a God perspective of our lives.

We need to have a God view of our lives not just the narrow view of things that are in front of us. Sometimes we view our lives with tunnel vision and the diagnosis looms over us day and night. What we choose to focus on is paramount to our healing and victory.

God looks at the valley and sees it as an opportunity for Him to comfort and strengthen us. It's a place where we learn to give our cares over to God; a place that builds character and causes us to grow beyond ourselves. If we will let Him, God will show us how to fight and persevere through impossible times. He will water the dry and parched valley and turn it into a blessing.

> *"I will make the wilderness a pool of water, and the parched land springs of water."*
>
> (Isaiah 41:18)

Is your soul dry and parched? Jesus offers you Living Water so you may take a refreshing drink and water your soul.

> *"Those who drink the water I give will never be thirsty again."*
>
> (John 4:14)

Keep praying God's Word into your circumstances and He will strengthen you to make it through! Remember, God is faithful and He watches over His word to perform it!

Chapter 14

Nevertheless – God!

Nevertheless is a word that God gave me an understanding of a number of years ago. It means that no matter what I am faced with, no matter how overpowering it looks, God has something to say about it.

For instance, when I was given the cancer diagnosis, I came to the realization that this was the doctor's report about my condition. But in my prayers and meditations God showed me that He also had a report for me. I learned to pray in such a way that God's report was overlaid on the doctor's report. The doctor's report was the fact of my diagnosis, but God's report was the truth about how God sees me. This is the "nevertheless" of God!

My prayer of faith became **"Lord, look what the doctor is saying about me. The diagnosis is cancer, but I want your word for me. I want to see the finger of God mixed with my faith which overtakes the doctor's report!"** God's report always trumps our bad report.

A STORY OF GREAT VICTORY

The Lord led me to the story of King Hezekiah in 2 Kings 19. It is a good example of the "nevertheless" of God. He was surrounded by the huge army of the Assyrians who had been fighting all the provinces and tearing through their armies like they were nothing. The King of Assyria sent a letter to Hezekiah stating their demands that Judah must surrender or be killed. The king knew that they were surrounded by an enemy that was mightier and more powerful than his smaller army. From his perspective of the facts, there was no way out. He knew that they faced certain annihilation, but then he took the letter up to the temple and laid it before the Lord.

He prayed a humble prayer which confessed that without God they had no hope. He pleaded his case before the Lord and ended with this request

> *"Now, O Lord our God, I pray, deliver us from his hand that all the kingdoms of the earth may know that You alone are God."*
>
> (Verse 19)

When I read this story, I identified with King Hezekiah. God showed me that the Assyrians represented the cancer cells that had me surrounded, and I of myself was powerless over the outcome, but my eyes were on God to rescue me.

The story goes on with King Hezekiah trusting in God to deliver them from their terrible enemy. God's response to that humble prayer was amazing!

> *"The angel of the Lord came in the night and cut down 185,000 Assyrians, and when King Hezekiah awoke in the morning not one of them was alive – all lay dead."*
>
> (Verse 35)

Some may call this a nice fairytale, but it is actually recorded in other historical secular books of biblical times and books of antiquities. The most well known reporting of the attack on Hezekiah is by the secular scholar Josephus recorded in his book Antiquities of the Jews – Book X, Chapter 1, Section 5. "God had sent a pestilential distemper upon his army: and on the very first night of the siege an hundred fourscore and five thousand, with their captains and generals, were destroyed." Assyrian history separately records this event in their accountings of this battle. The bible says "the angel of the Lord slew 185,000 in the night." Either way, King Hezekiah and all of Judah were saved. I call that tremendous answer to prayer! God moves in mysterious ways to help us when we cry out to Him.

The Lord quickened my heart to see that He would fight my cancer cells this way. That if I would give this report to Him, He would fight the battle for me. As I meditated on the stories in God's Word, I started to see many other stories where the odds were against the people, but God's intervention rescued them. This is the "nevertheless" of God. This story showed me that the facts that the doctor spoke to me were not the final verdict and that I should take it to the Lord, who is mightier and more powerful than any foe that I might face.

My faith started out as seeds but they grew huge during this season of cancer. The "nevertheless" of God is now firmly planted in me and no matter what I face, I want to see what God says about it.

GOD'S PLANS FOR US

Does it surprise you to know that God has a beautiful plan for your life? Since the day you were born, He has been with you guiding you every step of the way. Many times we don't hear Him, but He is always speaking to us.

> *"For I know the plans I have for you (Stephanie) plans to prosper you and not harm you; to give you a future and a hope. You will seek me and find me when you search for me with all your heart. I will be found by you."*
>
> (Jeremiah 29:11, 13)

This is a promise to all of us. You can insert your name into that promise!

When we battle with the promises of God on our side, victory is certain. God will accomplish in us what He promised. But victory in God's eyes is not always the way we picture it. At the time when I prayed for healing my idea of victory was that the cancer would be plucked out of my breast and I would have a miracle healing. I have actually seen those kinds of healings.

But as time went on, I could see that this was not how God saw my victory. Instead, as I opened the door with prayer, He came in and healed me on the inside first mentally, emotionally and spiritually. It was a season of learning how to trust God in ways that I never had to before, and then He healed me physically. He fully restored and strengthened me and grew my faith to such a degree that I will never be the same. That's complete healing!

THE MANY FACES OF FEAR

While going through cancer, I learned a lot about fear; what it is and what it isn't. It's natural for thoughts of fear to come when disaster strikes, but what we choose to do with those thoughts and how we entertain them on a daily basis impacts our quality of life, our ability to live in peace and our healing.

One day while I was praying I felt the Lord say to me **"Fear is but a vapor, it is nothing of itself."** In pondering this thought, I realized a simple but amazing truth; fear thoughts are nothing unless we allow them in! Fear itself is nothing, it needs someone to agree with it and entertain it, to focus energy on it for it to grow. Fear has no power on its own. Without a willing participant fear just evaporates! Remember the scripture I spoke about earlier? *"I have not given you a spirit of fear but of power, love and a sound mind."* *(2 Timothy 1:7)*

Replace fear with faith, replace fear with God's promises in the bible that bring peace, and fear will have no place to settle in you. Once we grasp this concept, we can say to disastrous circumstances **"I refuse to fear."** Our God is greater than any circumstance we may face.

Whenever fear thoughts tried to invade my mind, I would personalize God's Word like this based on Psalm 27 and pray:

> **"The Lord is my light and my salvation, whom (or what) shall I fear. The Lord is the defense of my life, whom (or what) shall I dread. The Lord is my strong shield and I am safe under His shadow."**

I prayed it as I drove to my oncologist or to chemotherapy and instantly peace would envelop me. Fear simply evaporates when faith meets it, like turning on a light switch; the darkness just vanishes. The word of the God spoken out loud was my weapon against cancer and fear thoughts.

Speaking the promises of God and personalizing them changes things within us. It changes the way we perceive our circumstances and how we respond to the things that side swipe us. We become saturated and immersed in God's presence and our mind, heart and emotions start to gain new faith. It changes our position to one of victory. **"I will not fear"** is a powerful statement in itself, but if we call on the name of the Lord as we speak, it becomes filled with the power of God to deliver us from the circumstances. **"I will not fear because it is the Lord my God who rescues me!"**

God will take you by the hand and walk you through whatever hard time you are going through. All that is needed is to ask Him, stand on His words of life and call them your own.

Again, this didn't happen all at once but it was little by little, day by day and it added up. The cancer diagnosis, surgeries and treatments that I went through lasted from June of 2005 through 2007 and after that every six months as I went in to get tested for the next seven years. God's Word sustained me through this whole process. It was a time of becoming intimately acquainted with my loving heavenly Father, my Lord and Savior Jesus and the words that are more than 2000 years old, yet fresh and powerful every day. God's Word breathed life into my soul, my heart and my mind. God's Word is timeless and eternal.

My hope is, if you are reading this book, that you will start applying these principles to your own situation. There is victory for you too!

Chapter 15

God's Ways are Higher

"The Lord is good, a stronghold in the day of trouble; and He knows those who take refuge in Him."

(Nahum 1:7)

How do we stand in the day of trouble? I call it contending, which I believe means pressing in fully to God day and night. We study His word and meditate on it until it is written in our hearts. And whatever happens, do not give in to cancer and every frightful thing that cancer brings with it. It means standing high above my problems with a God view of my life rather than my own small view; for His ways are higher than mine.

God says in Psalm 27 that He will hide us in His tabernacle and set us high above our enemies. He always has a new and fresh perspective for our circumstances.

How do we know this is so? By reading the Word which is the same yesterday, today and forever! The Old Testament is full of stories that pertain to our lives today. Usually that is not where we want to go when we read the bible. We are drawn to the lighter side, words of love and comfort.

However, when we are facing a giant like cancer or some other life threatening diagnosis, we are suddenly thrown into battle.

God's Word is where we learn how to fight our strongest enemies and gain victory. God always gives us the upper hand! Why? You are the apple of His eye!

> *"For he who touches you touches the apple of His eye."*
> (Zechariah 2:8)

THE MYSTERIES OF GOD

> *"The secret things belong to the Lord our God, but the things revealed belong to us and to our children forever"*
> (Deuteronomy 29:29)

There are mysteries that belong only to God and sometimes He chooses to reveal them to us, at the right timing. But there are things that we will never know or understand about God. If we learn to trust that God is faithful to His word, we can realize that we are not meant to know everything. Even the Apostles wanted to know about times and seasons and Jesus said to them,

> *"But of that day and hour no one knows, not even the angels of heaven, nor the Son, but the Father alone."*
> (Matthew 24:36)

God fights for us today, the same way He fought on behalf of Israel as they moved into the Promised Land and took new territory. God fights for us if we call upon Him. The Old Testament helps us to understand the nature of God. He is strong and fierce on our behalf and He will never leave or forsake us. It is written in the Old Testament and in the New Testament.

> *"I will be with you always until the very end of the age."*
>
> (Matthew 28:20)

> *"Be strong and courageous, do not fear nor be afraid; for it is the Lord your God who goes with you."*
>
> (Deuteronomy 31:6)

God the Father, God the Son and God the Holy Spirit (the Trinity) moves on your behalf and will never leave you alone!

Our God moves in mysterious ways as we pray and draw closer to Him. Little by little, day by day we can't help but learn to love Him and trust that He is our Lord and Savior, our deliverer and a God of restoration. He says if we search for Him with all our hearts that we will find Him and He will answer us. We begin to see there are so many aspects that we do not understand about God. He is greater than our mind can comprehend, yet as personal as our very breath.

The mysteries of God are supernatural in nature. Supernatural simply means above and beyond the natural or what our small human thinking can see or comprehend. As we come to understand that God is supernatural, that His ways really are higher than our ways, we start to gain greater faith that God can do anything! Yes anything!! God can and will move on our behalf, but we must learn how to ask.

SUPERNATURAL WAYS OF GOD

In reading the books of Exodus, Deuteronomy and Joshua, I started to see the supernatural nature of God to win my greatest battles. Exodus 14:14-19 speaks of the Angel of the Lord, the Pillar of fire and the cloud of glory. When the Egyptians were pursuing the Israelites and Moses was leading them out of Egypt, the Lord watched over them carefully. He instructed Moses continuously for the benefit of the Israelites.

When the Israelites were backed up against the Red Sea and all the people were afraid of Pharaoh's army which was pursuing them, God said

> *"Do not be afraid. Stand still and see the salvation of the Lord which He will accomplish for you today, and the Angel of God who went before the camp of Israel moved and went behind them; and the pillar of cloud went from before them and stood behind them. So it came between the camp of the Egyptians and the camp of Israel. Thus it was a cloud of darkness to the one, and it gave light by night to the other, so that the one did not come near the other all night."*
>
> (Exodus 14:13-19)

This is how the supernatural protection of God works, in ways that defy natural science and natural laws. We can't comprehend it, yet many of us have experienced the power of God moving on our behalf.

Is this merely a fairytale or a fable? I don't believe so. Years ago, I didn't really give it much thought and saw it as just another story in the bible. But when faced with cancer, I was drawn to these stories of battle and victory and they began to speak personally to my heart and circumstances. I saw how God can protect us against our strongest enemies in ways that we simply can't understand. God revealed some of His mysteries to me to grow my faith as I had need of it, and they belong to me forever.

EMBRACING GOD'S MYSTERIES

When God answered my prayer to heal my skin even though I was getting eight more radiation treatments, it was the unexplainable healing of God. When I was curled up on the sofa with no energy and He strengthened my body to go out and minister to others that was God's inexplicable strength in me. When my hair started growing back six days after my last chemotherapy treatment, it was the incomprehensible hand of God in my life.

All of these were examples of God's supernatural ability to heal me, which spoke to all the doctors, technicians and people who saw me go through this battle. It is the power of God to heal!

We have all heard stories of angels protecting people who would have died in an accident, or a warning received just in time from a stranger who was nowhere to be seen seconds later. I find it interesting how many people believe in the supernatural phenomena around us, but find it hard to believe in the supernatural of God.

Over a period of time I came to believe that if we can logically understand everything God does and how He does it, then He's not God! If you want God in a box, He won't do it! God wants a relationship with us, His beloved, but He doesn't need it. We do need Him but the sad thing is that sometimes we don't find Him. God says,

> ***"You will seek me and you will find me when you search for me with all your heart."***
>
> (Jeremiah 29:13-14)

He is standing right next to you at all times!

CLING TO THE LORD

God's Word says to "cling to the Lord" for strength in times of need. All of the places in the bible where it tells us to do this are usually in battle Scriptures. This is how we position ourselves for the victory! It is a place of safety.

The book of Joshua tells us

> ***"But you are to cling to the Lord your God, as you have done to this day. The Lord has driven out great and strong nations (enemies) from before you; for it is the Lord your God who fights for you, just as He promised you. So take diligent heed to love the Lord your God."***
>
> (Joshua 23 8-11)

What does God want from us? He wants our love; He wants our hearts to love Him.

So many times the bible tells us to love the Lord. Why? Because He loves us! He loves you not because of anything you have done, but because God IS LOVE; it is His very nature! God is not just loving; God is LOVE. This means He is the source of all love that is released to us, through us and throughout the whole world; a love so vast that man cannot comprehend it fully.

Here is a little of what God says about His love in 1 John 4:

"Let us love one another for love comes from God."

(Verse 7)

"Whoever does not love does not know God, FOR GOD IS LOVE."

(Verse 8)

"No one has ever seen God; but if we love one another, God lives in us and his love is made complete in us."

(Verse 12)

"God is love. Whoever lives in love lives in God and God in them."

(Verse 16)

We can see from these Scriptures that God is full of love for us and He desires our love. If we cling to Him like a child clings to a Father, God will move mountains on our behalf.

Deuteronomy 13:4 tells us to serve the Lord, fear Him (be in awe of Him), cling to Him; and Deuteronomy 10:20 says to worship Him, cling to Him! Why does the Lord want us to cling to Him? Because by doing so we will grow to trust His promises and His nature. We will be able to proclaim His promises over our own lives with confidence, and hold fast to Him and not give in to circumstances. It is a safe place for us.

One thing that made it easier for me to remain in God's peace was to listen to worship music at home and in the car. Worship music keeps our minds full of God's love rather than focusing on the problem. Cancer doesn't take a break, it just keeps on growing. So we can't afford to take a break. Resting in the Lord in calm confidence requires diligence and persistence.

Jesus said

> **"You shall know the truth and the truth will set you free."**
>
> (John 8:32)

This is so true, but the sad thing is we do not always learn what God's truth is and we remain in a state of fear, stress and chaos. This is not what God intended for us. Cling to the Lord and trust Him for full victory. God's Divine love for you has the power to crush your enemies and remove fear, doubt, anxiety and depression.

During my cancer season, I learned the principle of clinging to the Lord and abiding in Him daily. It became more and more natural for me to do it and as I did, I received increased peace and joy of the Lord in my heart and mind; I was set completely free from fear.

GOD IN THE MIDST OF US

Daily as I sought God's peace, it led me deeper into His Word and His presence. I definitely was not a bible scholar, and I had just started reading it for daily devotions a couple of years before cancer. But as I read it from a new perspective and a desperate point of need, a funny thing happened, each morning it was as if God was directing my reading to certain stories. He actually led me into many stories which I had never read.

These Old Testament stories were about war and how to fight our enemies; stories about how God fights on our behalf and soon they revealed more of Gods nature to me. I could see a theme throughout the stories which showed me God's desire to heal us and fight for us.

These stories reveal that God is fierce to fight on our behalf. He saves His vengeance for His enemies and, if we are His beloved children, our enemies are His enemies!

The New Testament Scriptures were about God's love, grace, mercy and forgiveness. They taught me about Jesus and His complete work on the cross, and His resurrection. I gained a deeper perspective on what Jesus did for me personally, as He poured out unmerited grace, mercy and favor into my life.

He wants to do this for all of us. But for some reason, Jesus is so misunderstood by our culture today and so misrepresented. At some point through previous generations, people started doubting the importance of Jesus in our lives, much like the Pharisees of His time in history. They doubted even though they saw first-hand miraculous healings. They spoke amongst themselves while plotting to kill Him. They were afraid that He would take away all of their position and authority. Some of them knew that Jesus was the true Son of God, but they crucified Him anyway. We must pray for personal revelation of who Jesus is to us!

DEALING WITH ANXIETY

> *"Do not be afraid nor dismayed because of this great*
> *multitude, for the battle is not yours but God's."*
>
> (2 Chronicles 20:15)

This is a truth that we must remember. Yes it is an accounting of someone else's story, but it is still the truth for us today! Truth is like a golden thread woven throughout the generations, unbreakable yet so misunderstood. No matter what generation they were originally spoken about, these are still words that God speaks to us today for our own battles. But our response is what causes God to move on our behalf.

What is your response when you read those words? Do you say "That was for then not for today?" Perhaps your response is "Lord I would like to believe, help my unbelief," or perhaps you agree with the words "Yes Lord I will call upon you to fight this battle for me." Different types of responses with very different outcomes!

The second response is one of a willing heart that wants to believe it. God can and will work with that to increase faith. The third response is one of agreement with what God says about how He will fight on your behalf! God always delivers on His word! The first response is a choice not to believe. In that case it would be good to pray for revelation of God's Word and its power for your life. He always wants to give us more revelation.

It is written various ways throughout the entire bible 365 times **"Do not fear, Fear Not, Be not afraid,"** both in the Old Testament and the New Testament. Usually if it is written about so much, it is important to God and to our well being.

BELIEVE AND PERSEVERE

In studying the battle Scriptures we see that we are to persevere in the day of trouble and not give in to the circumstances that come against us. We must stand on His promises for our future.

"Be anxious for nothing, but in EVERYTHING by prayer and supplication with thanksgiving (worship) let your requests be made known to God; and the peace of God which surpasses all understanding will guard your hearts and minds in Christ Jesus."

(Philippians 4:6-7)

Don't we need that kind of peace in our lives?

How many ways can God say that He loves us before we will comprehend the truth? God loves you just the way you are. You are the beloved of God right now. There is nothing that you can do to make Him love you more. If we turn our hearts to Him in prayer and thanksgiving, we open the door for Him to come into the middle of our circumstances and bring peace, joy, healing, comfort and life everlasting.

Unfortunately, many times it takes traumatic events to turn our hearts to God, to open the door through inviting His Son Jesus to come in to save us from destruction. It seems that we must reach the end of our rope before we ask for help. That's okay, whether it's cancer, other terminal diseases, loss of a loved one, severe depression or anxiety, whatever you are facing, God wants to comfort and strengthen you. He loves you more than you can even comprehend.

As I started to believe that God wanted to heal me in many ways other than just physical, I began to heal on many levels. Fear and anxiety are things that I wrestled with my whole life. You might say that I was a worrier!

I'm convinced that God knew this and He made His words come alive in my heart and mind to bring a peace that surpasses all understanding into the midst of the storm; then the healing began.

Little by little, my faith grew to greater proportions than I had previously experienced. God was there to comfort me and He is there to comfort you right this minute.

He is whispering in your ear *"Be still and know that I am God"* (Psalm 46:10) Trust Him to do what only He can do for you and be still. *"When the Lord delivers His promises He will give you rest on every side."*(Joshua 21:44) How wonderful is that! After we go through the storm clinging to the Lord with all our hearts, minds and strength, there is a time of rest and He will maintain our life with peace on every side. It becomes a time of victory over our circumstances, as we embrace the reality that God's ways really are higher!

> *"For My thoughts are not your thoughts, nor are your ways my ways, declares the Lord. For as the heavens are higher than the earth, so are My ways higher than your ways and My thoughts than your thoughts."*
>
> (Isaiah 55:8-9)

Chapter 16

Storms and Blessings

*"The Lord is my shepherd I shall not want. He makes
me lie down in green pastures, He restores my soul."*

(Psalm 23:1)

There is beauty to be found in the midst of the storms of life; blessings abounding in the middle of bad circumstances. God is the only one who can take us there.

In Psalm 23 just before it talks about the valley of the shadow of death, it speaks of repositioning us to a place where God can minister to us. This psalm refers to the Lord as our Divine Shepherd and tells us that no matter what, we shall not lack for any good thing.

Then God in His wisdom takes us to green pastures and makes us lie down; He leads us beside still waters and He restores our soul. All this BEFORE walking through the valley of the shadow of death! In this resting place before the storm, we learn to trust Him and then can proclaim:

*"I will fear no evil for You are with me. Your rod and
staff they comfort me"*

(Psalm 23:4)

Psalm 23 continues to tell us of a blessing place where a banquet table is prepared for us by our Lord and Savior, even in the midst of our enemies! It's a place where God anoints us with oil, He empowers us and pours out His blessing until it overflows.

> *"You prepare a table before me in the presence of my enemies; You anoint my head with oil; My cup runs over. Surely goodness and mercy shall follow me all the days of my life, and I will dwell in the house of the Lord forever."*
>
> (Psalm 23:5-6)

This is the resting place that God intends for us to battle from. You are welcome there any time. I encourage you to read all of Psalm 23 and proclaim it for yourself!

(A prayer from my journal)

"Lord only You can give me beauty in the midst of a cancer season; strength in the midst of the storm and a banquet table set before me in the middle of my enemies of fear, anxiety, death and destruction. Lord you set me in a large place and I feast on your unending love for me. I rejoice in the defeat of my enemies by your hand. Nothing is greater or stronger than my God! Thank you for rescuing me from the pit of destruction called "cancer." By your hand I am delivered into victory and a new blessing place! You are so good to me dear Lord, thank you!"

THE SUBSTANCE OF HIS WORD

God gave us His thoughts through the bible, the living Word. As I studied the bible from the desperate place of cancer, as I pressed into Him and let Him enfold me in His arms, His loving, rescuing, healing words overtook my fear. God's Word truly is the living Word, because its meaning is revealed in a greater way as we need it, when we go through hard seasons. When I learned how to personalize God's Word and soak in His presence, I became saturated with words of life and comfort. God continually revealed the application of His Word for my life over a period of years throughout the whole cancer process.

He will do this for you too. Just start right where you are and God will guide your heart.

BUILDING A FOUNDATION

Daily I called upon His promises over and over again. I spoke His words into my circumstances:

> *"Do not fear (Stephanie) for I am with you. Do not anxiously look about you for I am your God. I will save you, surely I will strengthen you, surely I will uphold you with my righteous right hand."*
>
> (Isaiah 41:10)

Words like these continually spoke to the very core of my soul. Where fear had been, there was a new peace and the dawning of a new faith that God actually loved me and would care for me. This belief became embedded in me no longer a new concept; it became mingled with who I am. Actually I would say that God's love unexpectedly overtook me and replaced the fear, doubt and unbelief that accompanied cancer with His view of my life. Again, this happened little by little, day by day forming a new deeper and more abiding relationship with Him.

The realization of the full impact of the cross became deeper and greater for me the more I embodied His word. The bible says that Jesus died for our iniquities and our sickness. That means God doesn't want me to be sick and He didn't make me sick. God wants to heal me and you!

> *"Bless the Lord O my soul and all that is within me; bless His holy name. Bless the Lord O my soul and forget none of His benefits, who forgives all your iniquities, who heals ALL your diseases; who redeems your life from destruction, who crowns you with loving kindness and tender mercies and satisfies your mouth with good things so that your youth is renewed like the eagles."*
>
> (Psalm 103:1-3)

Scriptures like this one reveal Gods nature towards us. He continually infused me with divine truth that I would not have encountered, if I had not had cancer and started studying His Words of love.

In actuality, going through breast cancer turned into the greatest season of blessing that I have ever experienced. God showed me that I am His daughter and that He would fight my battles for me. It became a season of repositioning me in Christ to receive all that God has for me. Think on this thought for a moment. What blessings could be in store for you, if you fully embrace Gods love and healing for your life even in the midst of the storm?

One thing I can guarantee is that you will never feel alone! It is God's good pleasure to reveal His unfailing love for us; and He pulls us in close to His side to shelter us from the storm. He will do that for you if you let Him.

DIVINE EXCHANGE

> *"To give them beauty for ashes, the oil of joy for mourning, the garment of praise for the spirit of heaviness."*
>
> (Isaiah 61:3 NKJV)

This is an example of God's divine exchange that He wants to give us. God wants to beautify our lives, to lift off the heavy burdens that we carry. Do you think He is judging you? No, He longs to have compassion on you! He weeps for His creation and longs to be gracious to us. God always wants to rebuild the ruins of our lives and give us life abundantly. Take a closer look at the Lord in His word; He wants to restore your life!

> *"Instead of your shame you will have a double portion and instead of humiliation they will shout for joy over their portion. Therefore, they will possess a double portion in their land, everlasting joy will be theirs."*
>
> (Isaiah 61:7)

This is the desire of God's heart for you. I encourage you to read all of Isaiah 61 to see His desire for your life.

God has a divine exchange for each of us if we will just ask Him. No matter what you are currently experiencing, God has a better plan for you. Open your heart and pray these words which are from His promises.

> **Lord you said you want to make an exchange with me; that if I lay down my burdens you will restore me. You said you want to give me beauty for the ashes of my life; you will give me the oil of joy for mourning, and the garment of praise for a spirit of heaviness. Lord you want me to be full of your joy for it replaces the sadness I have felt because of what I am facing.**
>
> **Lord right now I receive your divine exchange. Lord I love you and I praise you for being my light and salvation in the darkness. As I praise you and look away from cancer, sorrow and depression, as I stand in your joy and peace, you heal me from the spirit of heaviness that has wrapped itself around me.**
>
> **Lord I need your divine exchange in my life now. You Lord are my healer and I ask you to heal me from the inside out. Increase my faith to receive all that you have for me. Let me see the goodness of the Lord in the land of the living. Amen**
>
> (Isaiah 61:3, Psalm 27:1, 13)

Chapter 17

Speak Words of Life

God's Word is the most powerful medicine that we can give to our sick bodies and fearful minds. Drugs treat the symptoms, but God's Word goes deep down to treat our souls, our hearts and minds. All of these areas contribute to our health and sickness. If we will just read a little bit of God's word three times a day, we will see that it has the power to transform us and transcend our current difficulties.

When we find ourselves in the middle of one of life's storms, it is not natural to speak positive and reaffirming words. Many times a tragedy strikes and seems to come out of nowhere. It sideswipes us and knocks us down. The important thing is to get up and not stay down, this is a choice we must make. Speaking words of life to ourselves and our circumstances takes practice but it can be done. It becomes a discipline and a habit that we cultivate a over time.

We must carry the light of God's Word into every battle if we are to see victory. The light of God is like a sword that overpowers darkness.

Usually we start at square one unless we already have great faith to overcome the obstacle. Tragedy has a way of leveling the playing field and testing us all. In my case, speaking words of life meant praying and meditating on God's Word in my daily devotions, and then applying what I read to my own personal situation during the day.

WHAT GOD SAYS ABOUT HIS WORD

In this chapter I will share Scriptures that spoke to my heart and gave me great faith and courage to go through the cancer season without fear, and to walk in victory. Jesus speaks of relationship to the Father.

> *"In that day you will ask in My name, I do not say that I will request of the Father on your behalf; for the Father Himself LOVES YOU"*
>
> (John 16:26)

This Scripture tells us that God Himself answers us because He loves us!

He also said:

> *"I am not alone because the Father is with me. These things I have spoken to you, so that in Me you may have peace. In this world you will have trouble, but take courage for I have overcome the world!"*
>
> (John 16:32-33)

Jesus tells us plainly that He is not alone because the Father is with Him; and that we are to have peace in this. He has overcome the world for us and we will never be alone.

Do you want to be an overcomer? Do you want to walk in victory no matter what giant you face? Speak God's powerful Word into your situation and watch what He will do on your behalf!

WORDS OF LIFE SCRIPTURES

"Be gracious to me, O God, be gracious to me, for my soul takes refuge in You. In the shadow of Your wings I will take refuge until destruction passes by. I will cry to God Most High, to God who accomplishes all things for me. He will send from heaven and save me; He reproaches him who tramples upon me. God will send forth His loving-kindness and His truth."

(Psalm 57:1-3)

Cancer is the one that tramples on us like a bully, but God will hide us, heal us and save us! This is a Scripture of hope, faith and calm confidence that God will rescue us. Just speaking these words out loud begins to release a peace in me that God is in control of my situation and will rescue me from destruction.

"You have delivered my soul from death, indeed my feet from stumbling so that I may walk before God in the light of the living."

(Psalm 56:13)

Psalm 110 speaks of how we are to be positioned in Christ. He tells us:

> *"Sit at My right hand until I make your enemies a footstool. Rule in the midst of your enemies!"*
>
> (Psalm 110:1)

Jesus is seated at the right hand of God and we are positioned in Him, when we make Him our Lord and Savior. The Lord promises to give you, His beloved child, victory over your enemies! This Psalm was spoken by King David, but it is a truth for all believers. God wants you to be victorious over all your enemies and to dwell in peace as you rest in Him. Sit down and rest in Him, while the Lord cuts off your strong enemies.

> *"And (He) raised us up with Him, and seated us with Him in the heavenly places in Christ Jesus, so that in the ages to come He might show the surpassing riches of His grace in kindness towards us in Christ Jesus."*
>
> (Ephesians 2:6-7)

Again God shows us that we are seated with Jesus in a place of victory over all of our enemies! Cancer, terminal diseases, all fear, doubt, depression, oppression, addictions, sorrow and mourning; all of these are our enemies! Yet God wants us to rule and reign in the midst of our enemies. We need to get this truth in our hearts and minds that God wants us to be free. He is our strong tower and shield against destruction.

> *"From my distress I called upon the Lord; He answered*
> *me and set me in a large place! The Lord is for me; I*
> *will not fear."*
>
> (Psalm 118:5-6a)

He not only rescues you, but He sets you in a large place. God is on your side and He wants to help you live a larger, healthier and more prosperous life.

> *"You have been a refuge for me, a tower of strength."*
> (Psalm 61:3-4)

Say "Lord I take refuge in You daily."

CHOOSE LIFE ABUNDANTLY

In Deuteronomy God tells us to *choose* life.

> *"See, I have set before you today life and prosperity;*
> *and death and destruction, choose life in order that*
> *you may live, you and your descendants, by loving*
> *the Lord our God, by obeying His voice and holding*
> *fast to him."*
>
> (Deuteronomy 30:15)

> *"The enemy comes to kill, steal and destroy; but I have*
> *come that you may have life abundantly."*
>
> (John 10:10)

Life abundantly is God's will for you.

HEALING SCRIPTURES

> *"So shall My word be that goes forth from My mouth;*
> *it shall not return to Me void, but it shall accomplish*
> *what I please, and it shall prosper in the thing for*
> *which I sent it."*
>
> (Isaiah 55:11)

God declares that His word will not return to Him void. We are to pray His words back to Him by giving our voice to them, and He will deliver His promises into our lives. We are to speak the healing Scriptures out loud inserting ourselves into them. God's Word has power to heal, pray expectantly.

> *"He sent his word and healed them and delivered them*
> *from destruction."*
>
> (Psalm 107:20)

Ask the Lord to deliver you from all destruction.

Chapter 18

Examples of Healing

"A leper came to Jesus beseeching Him and falling on his knees before Him saying 'If you are willing You can make me clean.' Moved with compassion, Jesus stretched out His hand and touched him, and said to him 'I am willing, be cleansed.' Immediately the leprosy left him and he was cleansed!"

(Mark 1:40-45)

Jesus is moved to compassion when you ask Him with a humble heart to heal you. He says He is willing, are you willing to ask Him for your healing?

Jesus heals ten men who had leprosy.

"As He entered a village, ten leprous men who stood at a distance met Him and they called out to Him 'Jesus, Master, have mercy on us!' When He saw them, He said 'Go and show yourselves to the priests.' As they were going, they were cleansed. One of them saw that he had been healed and turned back glorifying God with a loud voice and fell on his face at His feet, giving thanks to Him; he was a foreigner. Then Jesus

answered 'Were there not ten cleansed? But the nine, where are they? Was no one found who returned to give glory to God except this foreigner?' And He said to him 'Stand up and go; your faith has made you well.'"

(Luke 17:12-19)

This Scripture demonstrates the importance of gratitude. I learned to speak my gratitude to the Lord for all that He was doing for me. Every time I became aware of answered prayer, I thanked Him for His faithfulness to me.

Another story that is filled with great faith for healing is found in **Luke 8:43, Matthew 9:20 and Mark 5:25**. Everyone was impacted by this healing miracle and it is recounted in three of the gospels.

"There was a woman who had been subject to a hemorrhage for twelve years. She had suffered a great deal under the care of many doctors and had spent all that she had, yet she continued to grow worse. She heard about Jesus and in her heart she thought to herself 'If I could but touch His robe, I will get well.' She made her way through the huge crowd and came up behind him and touched the fringe of His robe. Immediately the flow of her blood was dried up; and she felt in her body that she was healed of her affliction. Jesus perceiving in Himself that power had gone forth from Him, turned around and said 'Who touched My garments?' And He looked around in the crowd to see the woman who had done this.

But the woman fearing and trembling, aware of what had happened to her came and fell down before Him and told the whole truth. He said to her 'Daughter, your faith has made you well; go in peace and be healed of your affliction.'"

Here is a perfect example that shows us Jesus is a compassionate Savior who wants to heal us of all disease and bring us peace and comfort in our time of need. He is more than willing.

EXAMPLES OF HEALING TODAY

A friend of mine at church was diagnosed with cancer. The diagnosis was lymphoma, two tumors in one lung and a large mass in her chest. It was also in her lymph nodes! She stood in faith and declared that Jesus is her healer, praying daily in this way. She partnered with many people who prayed for her healing. Whenever she went back to the doctor he would always proceed to tell her that she still had cancer and she would say, "No I don't, Jesus is healing me!" She finally decided to go through the chemotherapy that the doctor insisted that she have.

However, after one chemo treatment, they decided to take a reading on the size of the tumors only to find out that they were completely gone! The doctors were dumbfounded as they compared the before and after ultrasounds. Daily she proclaimed "I am healed in the name of Jesus" and she received a miracle healing. I personally know this woman and she was amazed by what God had done for her. She also has the medical tests results as evidence. Her testimony continues to encourage many people and has opened the door for healing ministry.

Another man who was in our ministry training class was diagnosed with bone cancer just this past year. He and his wife went to a prayer group that has a lot of faith for healing and received prayer several times. They continued to pray in faith for healing, proclaiming God's Word daily. He is now walking in full remission of the bone cancer. His doctor is amazed and so are people around him. Praise God He still heals today!

GOD HEALS IN MANY WAYS

God never seems to heal in the same way, but He always heals. Healings happen in so many ways, and I have personally seen many varieties of ways that God heals.

God healed me over a period of time. Doctors, chemo and radiation were used in the process, but I ultimately came to believe that I would live. It is God who sustains my healing. But during the process, as I said previously, I was healed in many other ways before the physical healing manifested. I learned how to stand in faith and not allow fear to overtake me. I learned that I could have joy and peace of the Lord in any circumstance. Anxiety has no place in me because daily I turn everything over to God to handle. He knows the beginning from the end and He is faithful to complete what He started in me. He causes all things to work together for good in my life, even cancer!

Only God could heal my skin during radiation therapy when it was so burned and raw. My skin actually continued to heal and become perfectly normal as I received the last eight radiation treatments. That's the power of answered prayer!

Also the fact that my oncologist said it would be six weeks before peach fuzz would appear on my bald head, yet in six days after receiving prayer it started to sprout up and the doctor could not explain it. That's the power of answered prayer!

God strengthened me during all the chemotherapy to be able to be a leader in the ministry training class, on the prayer team, and to go to two prayer meetings per week to receive prayer that I needed for healing.

Many people who had seen loved ones go through the same treatments as me knew that something different was going on in me; as they had seen their loved ones shrivel and become weak and weary. God made me vibrant and alive and a walking testimony for the power of speaking His Word over cancer.

God didn't choose to treat me differently than others. I chose to stand on His promises and proclaim them in my life, and He was faithful to deliver me from destruction.

Chapter 19

Survive and Thrive

"For out of Zion will go the survivors! They shall take root downward and bear fruit upward. The ZEAL of the Lord shall perform it."

(Isaiah 37:31-32)

Cancer survivors are known as survivors of a mighty battle. Survivors against death and destruction; what could have happened did not happen. But I became acutely aware of a mindset among cancer patients as I went through the cancer healing process and even years afterward.

I had been speaking God's Word and promises over my life daily and I saw myself as healed. But when I met people who heard about me going through cancer, especially other cancer patients, they would inevitably ask me questions like "How long have you been a survivor?" and my answer was always "I'm not counting, I am healed."

After this happened a number of times, I began to realize that a large number of people who have gone through cancer and live to tell about it seem to gauge their lives around how long they have been a survivor.

There is nothing wrong with this in that it reminds them to live each day fully; it reminds them that they survived a huge whirlwind storm that many people do not. But once we get to the place of surviving the storm of cancer, I believe God has more for us. In the Scripture at the beginning of this chapter, God speaks of survivors and how He sees them. It is a picture of taking root and bearing fruit; a picture of a THRIVING! As I pondered this, I believe God said in my spirit, "You will not just survive, but now you will THRIVE."

It is true, we must survive all the hardship of cancer before we can thrive; but I also believe we must get past the mindset of just being survivors. When people ask me how long I have been a survivor, now I answer "I do not just survive, I thrive! Cancer is in my rear view mirror and I am healed!"

A survivor mentality keeps focusing our lives around the cancer season. It keeps us in a "cancer aware" mentality rather than a "completely healed" mentality. When the doctor says "Congratulations, you have now been cancer free for five years" or seven years that is something to celebrate. But we must move on from an attitude of just surviving and into an attitude of how to start thriving. Speaking words of life from Scripture is a great part of transitioning to thriving mode and maintaining that new position.

HOW DO WE MOVE PAST SURVIVOR MODE?

For me, the answer is centered in the Isaiah 37:31-32 scripture above; my view of my life, versus God's view of my life. Over the years of praying God's promises, I have come to realize that God's ways are really higher than my ways.

My view is a temporal view, whereas God's view is eternal. I now see that God's plans are much greater than mine, and He wants to use everything I've been through for good. A temporal view is a limited and narrow view of my circumstances. It is based on only what I can see in front of me at this minute, not on God's eternal plan and how it may be used to benefit the world around me. God always thinks bigger than us and His plan is always better! God says, in Isaiah 46:10 that he knows the end from the beginning. He knows everything about our future and He says He wants to help us.

How do we gain an eternal view of our lives when we can only see what we have survived; when we can only see what is in front of us? The answer is hidden in the mysteries of the bible. As we study God's Word in depth, His words become more personal and they permeate our hearts with faith. God's desire is to draw us closer to Him so we can start thriving right where we are. So we can start hearing and believing how much He, our creator, truly loves us.

Once again Jesus said

> *"I have come that you may have life more abundantly."*
> (John 10:10)

This is the key to thriving in this world. This is the key to becoming all that we were meant to be; to living a life that is bigger than us.

As we start listening to what God is saying to us and start applying it to our lives, we begin to thrive! God's Word waters the seeds of faith in our hearts and we begin to become fruitful.

This book was not my plan, it was God's plan. I am not naturally an author, but God in me is. What might you do with your experiences if you allowed God to transform your life? I believe what Jesus said is true **"but even if you say to this mountain 'Be taken up and thrown into the sea,' it will happen."** (Matthew 21:21) That's where my mountain of cancer is. It is not in me, but it is cast away from me.

115

This book is evidence to me that God has a larger plan for my life, and it does not involve living in fear of cancer returning. That to me is a temporal view or merely surviving in a fearful state. Cancer does not have a place in my life today except as words of encouragement to those going through it. We cannot take someone to a place where we have not gone ourselves. But after we have walked through the Valley of the Shadow of Death and survived, we can take others by the hand and lead them to victory. My hope is to lead thousands to victory, but the how and when is up to God!

DIFFERENT VIEWS OF VICTORY

Victory doesn't look the same for everyone. It is different for each of us, but it is real and it is there for you. Honestly, I have prayed for people with cancer who have died; and that broke my heart! But one thing I have seen over the years is that as I have worked with people for a period of time and brought them to prayer groups with me, the first thing that left them was paralyzing fear.

One man who was a friend of mine had terminal cancer. My husband and I took him and his wife to our prayer group to receive prayer for his cancer. An amazing thing happened. First their marriage was healed, as they had been on the verge of divorce. Love began to flow freely through their marriage and touched all of their children. Then fear of dying left him and peace overtook him.

He was not alone in his home at all. His men's group brought the meeting to his home weekly and they all bonded in love over that time. As his time drew near and we could see that he wasn't going to make it through the cancer, many of us went in teams or alone to pray for him and his wife. God poured out so much love and peace through friends that they were not alone.

The whole church even pitched in to do a dramatic renovation of their home so that they would be more comfortable. When he passed quietly and peacefully, we all saw the hand of God on it. It was apparently his time to go, but we all know that he is in heaven. His light still shines as an example of what God can do to bring healing in many areas during a time that can result in much fear and oppression. I call that victory over circumstances. It is victory over cancer and fear!

Ask God what He has in store for your life. How does He want to use you to encourage others and lead them to a greater place of peace? God wants to renew and restore your life and He wants all of us to become encouragers to help those who are going through the same experiences we have gone through. The Lord will bless you greatly if you have a heart to help others to experience victory over cancer and fear.

Chapter 20

Why Me God?

The mysteries of God cause us to ask "Why" in times of distress. Sometimes it seems so unfair that we would have to carry the burden, especially when we are trying our best to walk in His ways and to live a meaningful life immersed in His presence.

On December 7, 2012 I was once again given a cancer diagnosis for the second time. After seeing some sudden changes in my other breast, I went to my oncologist and they did a mammogram the same day and then an ultrasound. It was determined that I had another tumor and it had been growing undetected for quite some time. It also looked like an aggressive cancer again.

"Why me God?" It was my first response to this news. Wasn't the first time enough? I was alone when the doctor told me all of the findings, my husband was at work because I did not expect to be handed another cancer diagnosis that day. I went out to my car in shock and disbelief at this news and all I could do was cry. After composing myself, I called my husband and asked him to meet me so I could tell him.

When we met for coffee and I told him about the news, we both sat there in a state of stunned silence. We knew we had been here before, but this was different. We had already gone through the long season of breast cancer the first time and that was all behind us. It had been such a long battle, and the thought of having to go through it all again was almost unbearable.

In the days ahead there was some good news, if a cancer diagnosis can contain any good news. My first cancer had not metastasized, which would be the worst diagnosis. But this was a totally different kind of breast cancer, so they treated it as a brand new case of cancer. This time the diagnosis was estrogen and progesterone positive. The first cancer had been HER2 positive with no hormone receptor aspect to it. They gave me a hormone suppressant drug and no chemo or radiation was needed this time.

BREAKING THE NEWS

It had already been a difficult year. My father died of cancer six months before I received this news. Our twenty-one year old son was just coming home from the army for a month long Christmas break after serving in Afghanistan that year; and this was the news I had for him. My heart was breaking when I thought of how to tell my children once again that I had cancer. There is no easy way to say it and they were heartbroken over it. The first cancer was becoming a distant memory, as it had been seven years since my first diagnosis.

I asked the doctor if I could postpone the surgery until after the holidays when my son would be going back to his army post and he said I could. We scheduled the mastectomy for January 8, 2013.

STANDING ON GOD'S PROMISES

In those first few days after the diagnosis, I enquired of the Lord again and prayed **"God I need another promise to stand on, something that I can call on again to get me through this season. I can't**

do this without you!!" That prayer was my heart-cry to the Lord because I knew that I alone was not strong enough to go through this. The next morning as I opened my bible, it fell open to a Scripture I had never seen before. It almost jumped off the page at me,

> *"Not one of the good promises that the Lord made (to Stephanie) failed, all came to pass."*
>
> (Joshua 21:45)

My heart quickened when I read this and I just knew this was God answering my prayer quickly. What this did for me was to cause me to go through my old bible and go to each and every Scripture that God had given me as a promise during the first cancer season. Everything I read made my heart leap for joy!!

God is so good and He meets us right at our point of need. I am so grateful for that. After reading the new promise, my next declaration was to say, **"I refuse to fear cancer. Fear, leave me in the name of Jesus."** I was also reminded through God's word

> *"You will be far from oppression for you will not fear."*
>
> (Isaiah 54:14)

Going through my promises was a long process as I had received so many during the first cancer season. Now God was confirming to me that every good promise would come to pass. The other good thing that I could see was that it would take many long years for all of these promises to be fulfilled, and it reaffirmed this promise to me,

> *"I will live and not die to declare the works of the Lord."*
>
> (Nahum 1:9)

PREPARING FOR THE BATTLE

Once again I was seeking prayer from friends who had great faith for my healing. One word that I received from a friend was that this was going to be a much shorter season of cancer and that it would propel me to where God wanted to take me in ministry.

Now I don't for one minute believe that God struck me with cancer, but I do believe He knew it was going to happen. However, I also believe that He has a plan to use everything in my life for ultimate good.

This cancer season resulted in me writing another talk to share in Stonecroft Ministries about my breast cancer testimony. It also resulted in me writing this book *Victory Over Cancer and Fear.* I believe that God will use this book and my testimony to benefit many people and to encourage them to have hope and faith in something greater than themselves.

FACING THE CHALLENGES

After a wonderful Christmas season and many sweet family times with all of our kids, my son left to go back to his army post on January 5th and I was scheduled for surgery on January 8th. This time when they performed the mastectomy they also took a sample of my lymph nodes all in one surgery. There was no cancer in my nodes this time. The tumor was large again, about 3cm x 4cm Stage 2, invasive ductal carcinoma but it had not spread.

This time I opted for no chemotherapy or radiation treatment, as it was determined by an Oncotype DX test that it might not even be helpful at all. So I chose not to go through that again. They put me on Aromatase therapy to suppress the bad estrogen in my body and that was all.

During this second cancer season, my faith in God to sustain my life has grown even greater than it was before. Through reading Scripture, I have had a revelation that God is fully in control of how long I will live. My declaration is constantly

"I shall live and not die and declare the works of the Lord. I shall live out all the days that have been ordained for me in health, peace and joy."
(Psalm 118:17, Psalm 139:16)

I am still contending for my life today and I trust in God to deliver me from cancer; I am confident and at peace.

Nothing is allowed to rob me of the life that God has for me. Scripture says

"It rains on the just and the unjust alike."
(Matthew 5:45)

This means that life happens; I did not do something terrible which caused cancer in my body! We do know that as long as we are here on earth, we will go through troubled times.

The difference for me is that I have Jesus to call upon, a loving and compassionate Savior who will not leave me or forsake me ever. The Lord promises that He will be with us in trouble and even carry us when we grow weak; and He will always help us get to the other side of whatever valley we are trying to navigate.

This season is about me learning how to help and encourage others, who may have a similar diagnosis, to go through the process with the strength and hope of the Lord. I encourage you to lay down your heavy burdens at the foot of the cross and ask Him to take them from you. He always wants to exchange our troubles for His faith, hope, love and courage.

> *"He gives strength to the weary, and to him who lacks might He increases power."*
>
> (Isaiah 40:29)

I know this to be true because He has done it for me over and over again.

STANDING IN CONFIDENCE

As I write this book, I am reminded that I am going through the cancer season all over again. Some of you reading this are going through a similar season. The difference is we don't have to do it in fear. We can still live life abundantly; we can call upon the promises of God to deliver us from fear and anxiety; all we must do is ask Him with a smidge of faith.

If you want to start living victoriously and without fear, if you are ready to give up sorrow and pain, pray this prayer with me,

> **"Lord you said that you have come so that we may have life abundantly. This doesn't mean that we will never have trouble or sorrow, but I trust in you to lift off the heavy burden from my shoulders. Lord I'm asking you to help my mindset to shift to one of calm confidence and faith that you will strengthen me, that you will**

give me peace in the midst of my circumstances. Lord, I declare that you are in control; when I am weak you are strong.

Thank you that you sent your Light into the world to comfort us and take us out of darkness. I receive you Lord Jesus into my heart for you said '*I am the Light of the world He who follows me will not walk in darkness.*' I desperately need your light to flood into my circumstances and ask you now to enfold me in your arms, to deliver your promises of hope, peace and love into my life. Thank you, Jesus, for being my Lord and Savior. Amen"

He hears all your prayers and is ready and willing to step into your circumstances and cover you under God's great shield of protection. Also, I encourage you to read Psalm 91 daily, as it is filled with power to protect you and deliver you out of all circumstances that come against you. Pray this Psalm:

"He who dwells in the secret place of the Most High will abide under the shadow of the Almighty. I will say of the Lord you are my refuge and fortress, my God in whom I trust. For it is He who delivers you from the snare of the trapper and from the deadly pestilence. He will cover you will His pinions and under His wings you may take refuge. His faithfulness is your shield and bulwark."

(Psalm 91:1-4)

It also says that He will commission His angels over you to guard you in all your ways; they will bear you up in their hands so you do not stumble and fall. My husband and I read Psalm 91 and pray it all the time. It has become a "go to" Scripture for us.

Chapter 21

The Power of Praise

Heal me, O Lord, and I shall be healed; save me and I shall be saved; for you are my praise."

(Jeremiah 17:14)

Along time ago, someone ask me "If God is so almighty and powerful why does He need our worship and praise?" At the time I didn't know exactly how to answer that question. Now, years later after surviving many storms that life has thrown at me, I know how to answer that question.

God doesn't NEED our praise, we need to praise Him! When we sing praises to the Lord or meditate on His words, it fills us up with joy and peace! Praise connects our hearts with God and invites Him into our circumstances. Praise shifts our thinking and our hearts to be able to receive God's healing. Praise and worship is as powerful as prayer, sometimes I think even stronger.

In prayer and supplication we are to bring our requests to God, we are asking Him for something. But when we simply worship Him for His continual goodness, for His everlasting love and kindness our hearts open up and the love of God floods in and overtakes our problems. If we praise Him in the midst of the storm, His love will come in and calm the turbulence. His tremendous love for us will overtake us!

This is my strategy, praise the Lord in all circumstances. I turned my heart to the Lord even more than before, and He has been faithful to meet me there every day. When fear rushes in, as it still does, I stop and thank the Lord for saving my life, twice! I praise His holy name and thank Him for His Son Jesus who is with me always.

In the midst of a crisis ask the Lord for His help, but then praise Him that you know He will answer. Praise Him before the answer appears, before you can see it. Praise is like faith, it may not make sense at the time, but in the midst of the storm is when we need to do it. There is no storm too great for our God. Jesus is the name above all names; He is the name above cancer, He is the name above all disasters, He is the name above all disease. When we sing or speak of our thankfulness and sing to God's glory in our lives, the heavens open up and God's light, the Light of the World, floods into our circumstances.

Praise opens the door to Divine intervention for our problems. We pray for Divine Providence (God's hand in our circumstances) and then we worship with thankful hearts that His mighty hand will move in our circumstances.

Well, you may ask, how can I sing praises to Him if my loved one dies? God's Word says

> *"The Lord is near to the broken hearted and saves those who are crushed in spirit."*
>
> (Psalm 34:18)

Lean on Him and thank Him that He is near to you and trust Him to comfort you; then read His word and praise Him that He would never leave you nor forsake you. God will always get you through the sorrow, if you will ask Him.

One thing I truly believe is that God wants us to live all the days that were ordained for us and that none of those days should be robbed or cut short.

> *"Your eyes have seen my unformed substance, and in your book were all written the days that were ordained for me, before one of them came to be."*
>
> (Psalm 139:16)

When I pray according to God's will for me, I believe He will answer. His word says I will live out my length of days; that means I can pray that word over my life.

LIFE ABUNDANTLY

> *"The thief comes to kill, steal and destroy; but I have come that you may have life more abundantly."*
>
> (John 10:10)

Remember that "life abundantly" means life extravagantly! "Abundantly" to God is much greater than our small view of abundantly. The definition in Strong's Concordance says the word abundantly is taken from the Greek word *'perissos'* which means "superabundance, excessive, over and above, overflowing, more than enough, profusely, above the ordinary more than sufficient."

God's idea of abundantly is more than we can imagine. Jesus said that He came so we may have life MORE abundantly! That is huge, and if we tap into it and speak it into our circumstances, God can move mountains out of the way. God can heal cancer and He can certainly comfort us. As we read about these things, we slowly begin to trust God, His nature and His intention towards us.

THERE IS GOOD NEWS

God sent His only son to bring the good news to us about His never-ending love and that He wants to be part of our everyday lives. Jesus spoke what He heard the Father saying.

> *"If you have seen me, you have seen the Father. For I am in the Father and He is in me."*
>
> (John 14:11)

When we are faced with disaster or even everyday situations, we must stop and examine what the bible says about it. Then we can pray effective prayers from God's Word over the situation and watch and see the Lord move on our behalf. Praise and worship daily sets our hearts right so we can quickly move into prayer at any given moment.

You will find that the more you sing or speak praises to the Lord, the more peace you will have and the joy of the Lord will fill your heart and mind. When I am filled with the peace and joy of the Lord, all my enemies including fear, anxiety, stress and negative thoughts melt away. Then I walk in life abundantly and it becomes my new address. I choose to dwell in life abundantly!

Pray from the Scriptures in Isaiah and personalize it like this

> **"Lord, you are my salvation, my strength is in you God; you are my song and with joy I draw water from the wells of salvation. I praise you and tell everyone of your goodness. I sing to the Lord for He has done excellent things. Everytime I sing, energy, joy and the peace of the Lord, fills me up to overflowing and my enemy (cancer) melts away! Thank you Lord. Amen"**
>
> (Isaiah 12:2-6)

In the next chapter I will share more Scriptures that are meant to encourage, strengthen and comfort you.

Chapter 22

Words of Life Scriptures

These Scriptures can be personalized by inserting your name and circumstances in them. As you speak them out loud and dwell on their meaning, you will gain new faith and hope that God will deliver you from your troubles. Faith is cultivated like a garden, it does not come naturally. For some reason fear comes quickly as we look at our circumstances. I think this is so because we see the evidence of bad things with our eyes.

We cannot see faith, so it must be grown a little at a time. The faith you build today will carry you through tomorrow's storms. As we cultivate faith, it becomes our new default mode. Meditate on these Scriptures day and night and you will grow your faith.

> *"He who dwells in the secret place of the Most High shall abide under the shadow of the Almighty. I will say of the Lord, my refuge, my fortress, my God in whom I trust; for it is He who delivers you from the snare of the trapper and the perilous pestilence."*
>
> (Psalm 91:1-2)

I pray Psalm 91 daily so that I can get a mental picture of dwelling with and abiding in God Almighty who rescues me.

"No evil will befall me neither shall any plague come near my dwelling. For You have given your angels charge over me. They keep me in all my ways."

(Psalm 91:10-11)

"In my pathway is life, healing and health."

(Proverbs 12:28)

"When he falls, he will not be hurled headlong because the Lord is the one who holds his hand."

(Psalm 37:24)

Though life may knock me down, I will not hit the ground because my loving Father God holds my hand and my loving savior Jesus guides my path.

"The Lord is my light and my salvation, whom shall I fear? The Lord is the defense of my life, whom shall I dread? When evildoers (cancer) came upon me to devour my flesh, my adversaries and my enemies they stumbled and fell. Though a host encamp against me, my heart will not fear; though war arise against me, in spite of this I shall remain confident."

(Psalm 27:1-3)

"For in the day of trouble (doctor's diagnosis and fear) He will conceal me in His tabernacle; in the secret place of His tent He will hide me. He will lift me up on a rock."

(Psalm 27:5)

"I would have despaired unless I had believed that I would see the goodness of the Lord in the land of the living."

(Psalm 27:13)

He will lift me up high above my enemies always and I will sing for joy that the Lord has protected me. I will have courage and faith that I will see His goodness in my circumstances.

"When I am afraid, I will put my trust in You; in God whose word I praise. In God I have put my trust; I shall not be afraid. What can mere man do to me?"

(Psalm 56:3-4)

Also, what can a doctor's report do to me when I am protected by my God? Remember there is the doctor's report and then God's report.

"For You have been a refuge for me, a tower of strength against the enemy. Let me dwell in Your tent forever; let me take refuge in the shelter of Your wings."

(Psalm 61:3-4)

"Bless the Lord O my soul and all that is within me, bless His holy name; Who forgives all your iniquities, who heals all your diseases, who redeems your life from destruction, who crowns you with loving kindness and tender mercies, who satisfies your mouth with good things, so that your youth is renewed like the eagle's."

(Psalm 103:1-5)

Isaiah 40 speaks about the raw power of God to move in all circumstances in the earth. Then He personalizes it:

> *"He gives strength to the weary, and to him who lacks might He increases power. Though youths grow weary and tired, and vigorous young men stumble badly; yet those who wait for the Lord will gain new strength; they will mount up with wings like eagles. They will run and not grow weary, they will walk and not faint."*
>
> (Isaiah 40:29-31)

> *"Do not fear for I am with you; do not anxiously look about you for I am your God. I will strengthen you, surely I will help you, and surely I will uphold you with my righteous right hand."*
>
> (Isaiah 41:10)

Pray this when fear and anxiety arise.

> *"Do not fear, for I have redeemed you. I have called you by name; you are Mine! When you pass through the waters, I will be with you; and through the rivers, they will not overflow you. When you walk through the fire, you will not be scorched, nor will the flame burn you; for I am the Lord your God, the Holy one of Israel, your Savior."*
>
> (Isaiah 43:1-3)

God tells us all through the bible "do not fear" because He is with us in every battle and victory. We will not drown when the waters threaten to overwhelm us, we will not be scorched when we are thrown into the fire. Stand and see the saving power of the Lord on your behalf.

> *"And great multitudes followed Him, and He healed them ALL."*
>
> (Matthew 12:15)

> *"And when Jesus went out He saw the great multitude, and He was moved with compassion for them, and healed their sick."*
>
> (Matthew 14:14)

> *"Then Jesus answered and said to her, "O woman, great is your faith! Let it be to you as you desire, and her daughter was healed from that very hour."*
>
> (Matthew 15:28)

God loves a faith filled heart. Pray in faith and see what God will do.

> *"And the whole multitude sought to touch Him, for power went out from Him and healed them all."*
>
> (Luke 6:19)

> *"Then He called His twelve disciples together and gave them power and authority over all demons, and to cure diseases. He sent them to preach the kingdom of God and to heal the sick."*
>
> (Luke 9:1-2)

"Whatever you ask in My name, this I will do, that the Father may be glorified in the Son."

(John 14:13)

"Is anyone among you sick? Call for the elders of the church, and let them pray over him anointing him with oil in the name of the Lord - And the prayer of faith will save the one who is sick, and the Lord will raise him up.

(James 5:15)

"And this is the confidence we have toward Him, that if we ask anything according to His will, He will hear us."

(1 John 5:14)

You can see the pattern in these Scriptures; God wants to heal us! Jesus healed all who came and asked. His healing touch is available to all of us and He invites us to come to Him and ask. Healing doesn't always look the way we think it should, but God wants to heal every part of us from the inside out.

It is God's will for us to be healed of sickness and to have victory over our battles. I have seen so many healings over the years that I can't count them all. God's Word shows His heart for us and that He is on our side! Here are just a few of the Scripture from The Book of Acts.

The Book of Acts shows the Glory of God being released through the Apostles. A man who was lame from birth used to be carried to the gate of the temple daily where he would beg for money.

"Peter said to him 'Silver and gold I do not have, but what I do have I give you. In the name of Jesus Christ of Nazareth, rise up and walk.' He took him by the right hand and lifted him up and immediately his feet and ankle bones received strength."

(Acts 3:2-8)

"Also a multitude gathered from the surrounding cities to Jerusalem, bringing sick people ... and they were all healed."

(Acts 5:16)

"Now God worked unusual miracles by the hands of Paul, so that even handkerchiefs or aprons were brought from his body to the sick, and the diseases left them ..."

(Acts 19:11,12)

"He sent His word and healed them, and delivered them from their destructions."

(Psalm 107:20)

"I shall not die, but live, and declare the works of the Lord."

(Psalm 118:17)

Choose to live and to fight the good fight!

"I have set before you life and death, blessing and cursing; therefore choose life that both you and your descendants may live."

(Deuteronomy 30:19)

God's Word will not fail you.

"Not a word failed of any good thing which the Lord had spoken . All came to pass."

(Joshua 21:45)

Jesus bore your sins and sickness. He willingly died on the cross for all of us to blot out the sins of the world.

"He was wounded for our transgressions, He was bruised for our iniquities; the chastisement for our peace was upon Him, and by His stripes we are healed."

(Isaiah 53:5)

His stripes on His back were born for us and when He said "It is finished" on the cross, He gained power over darkness for all of us. We are set free.

Speak to the mountain of sickness:

"Have faith in God. For assuredly I say to you, whoever says to this mountain, 'Be removed and be cast into the sea,' and does not doubt in his heart, but believes that those things he says will come to pass, he will have whatever he says."

(Mark 11:22,23)

Again, Jesus is telling us to speak words of life. Say to your mountain of sickness, finances, emotional pain "Be removed and be cast into the sea," and it will be done for you.

Above all else remember to proclaim this often.

"The Joy of the Lord is my strength!"

(Nehemiah 8:10)

In the midst of our sorrow, sickness, depression; this is a powerful statement! I say daily **"The Joy of the Lord is my strength."** And it has become so.

Chapter 23

Contend for Your Healing

When we are contending for a huge move of God in our lives, we don't just speak it once and say "OK I did it." No! We speak it day and night, building up our faith until we see it manifest in our lives. We pray and then stand; we pray and are strengthened; we pray and receive peace. We contend for a season until we see the healing manifest. Cancer never takes a break so we must press in to God continuously!

We daily thank God that He is moving on our behalf even if we don't see it yet. We give thanks that He created us to be in perfect health and thank Him that He is restoring us.

God is in the business of healing His people today, and it is His will to see you walk in health and freedom. This pertains to healing of all kinds including addictions or any other enemy you may be battling. Contend for the divine move of God on your behalf and you will see that He can deliver you from anything that you may be facing. Nothing is too great for our God!

In the words of Jesus:

"Peace I leave with you, My peace I give unto you, not as the world gives, give I unto you."

(John 14:27)

Contact the Author

To schedule a speaking event at your church, a conference, retreat or seminar, please contact me at the email address below.

For large quantity book orders please contact us by email or on the website listed below.

Email: wordsoflifeministry@outlook.com
Website: wordsoflifeministryusa.com

Also, I welcome any personal testimonies or stories you may want to share with me.

Blessings to you on your journey to health, peace and joy!